Tony Vinmin tes

The world of 1980s fashion illustrator
TONY VIRAMONTES

BOLD, BEAUTIFUL AND DAMNED

DEAN RHYS MORGAN

FOREWORD BY
JEAN PAUL GAULTIER

LAURENCE KING PUBLISHING

PAGE I
A FLUID INTERPRETATION OF
A MILITARY CAP IN BOWLER
FELT BY HALLELUJAH
BOULEVARD FOR BRITISH
VOGUE. PARIS, 1983.
VOGUE © THE CONDÉ NAST
PUBLICATIONS LTD

PAGE II
LESLIE WINER, IN A GRAHAM
SMITH HALO HAT, APPEARED
IN THE DECEMBER ISSUE OF
BRITISH *VOGUE* IN A
FEATURE CELEBRATING
'THE NEW FEMME FATALE'.
PARIS, 1983

PAGE V
LISABETH GARBER. PARIS,
1983

PAGE VI
RON GRACE DRAWN FOR THE
COVER OF *LE MONDE*. PARIS,
1986

ENDPAPERS
A SELECTION OF POLAROIDS
TAKEN BY TONY
VIRAMONTES IN THE 1980S

LAURENCE KING

Published in 2013 by Laurence King Publishing Ltd
361–373 City Road
London EC1V 1LR
United Kingdon
Tel: +44 20 7841 6900
Fax: + 44 20 7841 6910
email: enquiries@laurenceking.com
www.laurenceking.com

© 2013 Laurence King Publishing
Unless otherwise stated, all images are courtesy of the Tony
Viramontes Studio Archive.
This book was produced by Laurence King Publishing.

Copyright © text 2013 Dean Rhys Morgan
Dean Rhys Morgan has asserted his right under the Copyright,
Designs and Patent Act 1988, to be identified as the Author of
this Work.

ISBN: 978 1 78067 307 3

Printed in China

CONTENTS

FOREWORD BY
JEAN PAUL GAULTIER

I immediately spotted the remarkable talent of Tony Viramontes. In particular, the series of advertisements he produced for the Genius Group as well as the black-and-white images with newspaper hairdos entitled Headings that were published in *Jill* magazine in September 1985: magnificent black-and-white images that were striking in their intensity and graphic quality.

I was struck by this world that corresponded so closely to the creative avenues that I myself was pursuing at the time. Notably his choice of models. In fact, a number of models who appeared in my catwalk shows in the 1980s also featured in Viramontes's images: Tanel Bedrossiantz, Claudia Huidobro, Laurence Treil, Ben Shaul, Mike Hill, Anthonis, Nick Kamen, Violeta Sanchez, Walter, Mimi, Christine Bergstrom, Talisa Soto, Teri Toye.

Tony Viramontes's influence was so great and his style so powerful that they have left their mark on the period and on fashion.

A shooting star who was able to unite in a single image several diverse elements: photos redrawn or highlighted in marker pen (a genre that he initiated and went on to pioneer), illustration, collage, design, graphics and finally FASHION.

Unlike many other artists and photographers, he really loved, adored and worshipped fashion! It was almost a form of social activism, enabling him to express himself through his works.

His images will remain symbolic of the 1980s but have also become classic examples of a timeless modernity.

Jean Paul Gaultier
Paris 2012

OPPOSITE: **FACE FORWARD** VIRAMONTES TAKES THE IMPACT OF BLACK TO A WHOLE NEW LEVEL IN THIS CHARACTERISTICALLY GRAPHIC SKETCH OF A FELT HEADDRESS BY STEPHEN JONES FOR JEAN PAUL GAULTIER'S SPRING/SUMMER COLLECTION. PARIS, 1984

OUR BROTHER TONY

Had he lived, Tony would have been 56 this year. In the 25 years that have passed since his death we have often wondered what he might have been doing today. When Dean asked us to write a few words about our younger brother it was a bitter-sweet moment, as Tony's life was in many ways defined by his early death. He experienced a lot in his 31 years and had a full-colour paint box, which made him a really special person.

What was he like? Well, Tony was always a bit of a maverick; he had a great energy about him, he was curious about life, loved to be around his family and fed off his environment. He knew he was good at what he did, but he could perhaps have afforded to be more confident. He could be a little shy, but once he let you in you couldn't stop him talking about all the things he loved – like fashion, art and music.

Like us, he was always very passionate about what he did, and he really wanted everything to be perfect. Tony chose to live his life according to his own set of rules and had his own unique perception of the world. As we get older we see the influence of our brother's work all around us and we are grateful to Dean Rhys Morgan for bringing together the many threads of his life and work in this long-overdue and beautiful book.

Ed, Ralph and Manuel Viramontes
Los Angeles, 2012

ABOVE: **TONY VIRAMONTES** PHOTOGRAPH BY ED VIRAMONTES. PARIS, 1986

OPPOSITE: **SLEEK CHIC** VIRAMONTES EVOKES THE IMPRESSION OF AN ART DECO HEROINE IN THIS UNCHARACTERISTICALLY POLISHED COVER IMAGE FOR *HAMPTONS* MAGAZINE. NEW YORK, 1982

OVERLEAF: SYLVANA CASTRES LOOKS ON AS VIRAMONTES COMPLETES A STUDY OF MODEL TERI TOYE IN HIS TINY NEW YORK APARTMENT BEFORE LEAVING THE CITY FOR PARIS. PHOTOGRAPH BY JEAN-JACQUES CASTRES. NEW YORK, 1963

INTRODUCTION

I never met Tony Viramontes, though I have long been familiar with his work: from the sweeping, hedonistic images he created for the pages of *La Mode en Peinture* to the darkly romantic sleeve art for Arcadia's 'So Red The Rose'. But I knew very little about the man himself. A conversation with illustrator David Downton in October 2008 prompted an initial web search, which raised far more questions than it answered. More than 20 years after his death, Tony Viramontes – this master of descriptive line who captured the pulse of the 1980s so effortlessly – is a forgotten figure in the history of fashion illustration.

Overshadowed during his lifetime by his friend and mentor Antonio Lopez, with whom he shared a certain street sensibility, Viramontes has gradually and unaccountably slipped from view. There has been the occasional resurgence of interest in his work. The advent of the Internet, Facebook and blogging brought forth a flurry of images and anecdotes, though most of the published material is biographically thin, anecdotal and often simply inaccurate.

While the intention of this book is not to set out a definitive biographical study of Tony Viramontes and his work, my hope is that it provides a clear introduction to the people he knew and the work he produced during his short but prolific career. He was well enough known in his own lifetime to become the voice of countless magazine and advertorial pages. Perhaps the reason for the neglect that has followed is not just the fickleness of public attention, but the fact that Viramontes (as he always signed his work) was an artist who chose to make his career – and earned his subsequent reputation and celebrity – in the rarefied world of fashion and haute couture. He was that rare and now all-but-extinct beast, a fashion illustrator.

Fashion illustration today does not enjoy the key role it did during its heyday in the 1940s and 1950s, when glossy magazines were filled with stylized sketches of rather startling looking women. By the time Viramontes made his *New York Times* debut in 1979, fashion illustration had not been fashionable for some time. For the previous two decades, Antonio Lopez had been the only artist given regular commissions. Viramontes followed Lopez in making fashion illustration contemporary and accessible. Paradoxically, Tony was both a

link in a long illustrative tradition and a startling original. While his figures were elongated and slender, as was traditional in fashion drawing, his work lacked many of the clichés that populated the aristocratic drawings of old. He quickly caught a wave as Prosper Assouline began editing the illustration-only title *La Mode en Peinture* and in 1980 Anna Piaggi took her appetite for the painted page to Condé Nast, where she curated the avant-garde journal *Vanity*. For a brief period, Tony was at the centre of the fashion world.

Fashion illustration has long struggled to be taken seriously, against a prevailing view that the artist comes by the material second-hand, merely drawing a picture to represent someone else's idea, rather than contributing an underlying intellectual argument or comment on the culture that produced it. Tony's celebrity lasted just as long as his work continued to appear in print; when it ceased to appear, the name Viramontes was quickly forgotten and the world moved on. A posthumous exhibition of his drawings in Paris at the Ménagerie de verre in October 1991 was his sole memorial. Many drawings have since disappeared or fallen into anonymity. Some of his sketches passed into the collections of his friends and acquaintances, a few were sold to collectors and some made their way into the archives of the fashion houses for which they were created. The remainder were packed up and shipped off to his family home in Los Angeles where they have remained untouched and unseen.

Yet Tony's images are as fresh and compelling now as they were nearly 30 years ago and a large part of the impetus behind this book has been to reintroduce his work, to bring it to a new generation of fashionistas. His family gave enthusiastically of their time as I attempted to piece together the story of Tony's life. After we struck up an email correspondence in 2010, Tony's older brother Ed Viramontes invited me to take a look at his brother's work. I went. I saw. And I was conquered. In the age of computer-generated imagery, drawing has for a time been considered a laughably anachronistic medium, but today is enjoying a resurgence. The skilled use of line has long held the credential of being one of the most effective artistic methods to convey emotion. Drawing is direct and opinionated. Tony was an artist who drew and made sketches almost constantly throughout his life. I have always admired

originality, and there are certain artists whose personas inform their work and make it immediately recognizable. Tony's work – despite a variety of visual idioms – always bore an unmistakable hallmark. Whether in carefully controlled line drawings, subtle washes of colour or bold elemental brushstrokes, whatever the technique the handwriting was always uniquely Viramontes.

Over the course of the next year I got to know Tony through the eyes of his friends and loved ones, as I worked my way through the better part of almost a thousand pieces of artwork, all carefully preserved by Ed and his family. It was during this process that I became aware of the scope, breadth and richness of his short career. Tony's output was staggering: for every approved or published drawing he made there might be ten or 12 alternatives. Additionally, there were piles of old newspapers and magazine clippings, sketchbooks, scraps of paper, photographs, correspondence and diaries. Tony left quite a trail and while his diaries are neither chronological nor particularly literary they nevertheless constitute a strong personal document, in which he recorded his many observations on his own character and achievements in a wild jumble of words on work, love, childhood and hats!

A large part of the joy in compiling *Viramontes* was the opportunity to meet so many people I have long admired. Indeed, a great many people assisted in the creation of this book by sharing memories, loaning art, making introductions and allowing me into their archives of both words and pictures, enabling me to reconstruct Tony's history. I travelled to Paris, Rome and Los Angeles to interview the people who had known and worked with him. One of the best tributes that one can pay to Tony Viramontes is that his friends (and indeed the occasional foe) loved to talk about him. His close friend, model agent Cyril Brulé, remembers Viramontes as someone 'who held an enormous fascination for people'. If I have managed to capture but a portion of his captivating personality and drive then my work will not have been in vain. For no history of twentieth-century fashion illustration would be complete without recognizing Tony Viramontes.

Dean Rhys Morgan
New York, 2012

VALENTINO
HAUTE COUTURE
BOLD AND GRAPHICALLY
DARING, VIRAMONTES
WORKED AT FULL VELOCITY
AND TOOK COMMAND OF
THE PAGE WITH COMPLETE
ASSURANCE. THIS TYPICALLY
DYNAMIC SKETCH WAS ONE
OF A SERIES FOR VALENTINO
HAUTE COUTURE. ROME,
1985. COLLECTION OF
VALENTINO GARAVANI

14

PORTRAIT OF AN ARTIST

'Draw for yourself, paint for yourself, take photographs for yourself, you will love them much more.'

VIRAMONTES

If Tony Viramontes had never existed, he would certainly have been imagined: a complex and nuanced figure, a street-smart dandy who played the part to the hilt, but at the same time fickle and contradictory, a visionary too far ahead of his time. A man of an avid and frenzied modernity, living at breakneck speed, everything about Tony was quick: the way he thought, the way he drew; he had instant ideas.

To work, he needed a model, he needed music, he needed everyone in the room – he wanted that electricity. What most people consider distractions Tony Viramontes used as fuel. Sitting with a board propped up on a table, he would fire off hundreds of sketches, throwing them over his shoulder as he went, leaping effortlessly from one graphic frolic to the next, as he conjured up his scowling models with their flashing eyes and scornful red lips.

It must have been a revelation to watch the images spring forth from his hand. Tony drew in charcoal – quick, clean, decisive lines made with small thin sticks. 'It is essential to capture the image; not a detail, not a garment or an expression, but an impression. Of the hundreds of sketches I might make for one drawing, it's almost always the first that states the essential.' For Tony Viramontes fashion was an idea, a score to be settled, a drawing to be coloured with his imagination.

Frank Anthony Viramontes was born on 8 December 1956, in Santa Monica, California, to Anita and Frank Viramontes. Both parents were the offspring of first-generation Mexican immigrants. His mother's family hailed from Guanajuato, while his Dad's parents were from a small town called Tequila.

Tony's parents were members of the careful middle classes. Frank was a machinist for the McDonnell Douglas Aircraft Company and Anita worked for the telephone service AT&T. Home was Beloit Avenue, located in the suburbs of West Los Angeles, where Tony's parents provided him with a good Catholic upbringing and an idyllic all-American childhood. He was the third of four siblings – Manuel, Ed, Tony and Ralph. Frank and Anita were extremely supportive and nurturing of all their boys, despite their very obvious differences. Manuel, Ed and Ralph were athletic; Tony exhibited a strong artistic streak and spent most of his time drawing. He began by documenting his brothers' football games and progressed to marching bands and cheerleaders. Anita, who had a sophisticated appreciation of art, encouraged her son's nascent talents, which for a period included drawing bullfights. Tony was about ten years old when his parents began taking him to the old bullring in Tijuana, Mexico. Right in the middle of the town, it once drew Hollywood starlets such as Marilyn Monroe and Ava Gardner to its stands. Tony found the sense of pomp and pageantry around the ring intoxicating and while his family watched the fight unfold he would sketch the performance. Even in childhood Viramontes had an eye that missed nothing and pieced together his perceptions in a highly personal way. Years later he recalled in detail the brightly coloured, gilt-edged uniforms of the *toreros*, the rush of the music, the passion of the crowd. 'It was all so beautiful,' he said, 'a complete source of artistic inspiration.'

Tony's early choice of subject was to prove symptomatic of his later love of fashion and the way in which his eye was drawn almost magpie-like to glittering surfaces. Anita believes it likely her third son, so different from his brothers, inherited his love of fashion from her. 'He was always very interested in clothes and would often notice what I was dressed in,' she recalls.

ABOVE: **STEVEN MEISEL,**
c. 1979, AND **TERI TOYE,**
c. 1985. POLAROIDS BY
VIRAMONTES

OPPOSITE: **TERI TOYE**
DRAWN FOR THE COVER
OF *HAMPTONS* MAGAZINE.
NEW YORK, 1983

PREVIOUS PAGE: **TONY VIRAMONTES**
FASHIONABLE TO THE END, TONY
COMMISSIONED ALICE SPRINGS
(MRS HELMUT NEWTON) TO SHOOT
THIS PICTURE WHILE ALREADY
SUFFERING FROM THE ILLNESS
THAT TOOK HIS LIFE. MONTE
CARLO, 1986. © ALICE SPRINGS /
MACONOCHIE PHOTOGRAPHY

By his teens, Tony's drawings were dominated by women; the fashion illustrator Antonio Lopez was one of his biggest inspirations. He began persuading high school friends to pose for him. 'I was Tony's first muse,' remembers classmate Julie Rosenbaum. 'I was like his little doll. When we got together he would put on my make-up, style my hair and shoot pictures of me.' Rosenbaum was one of the first people to recognize Tony's talents and she encouraged him to take an art class. However, she was quickly replaced as muse when Viramontes 'became enamoured by a model named René Russo'.

After high school Viramontes attended the Art Center College of Design in Pasadena, from 1972. It was there that one of his instructors, Paul Jasmin, told him that if he wanted to study fashion illustration seriously he should go to New York. Two years later – by now the late 1970s – he moved, staying at the YMCA and then the infamous Chelsea Hotel before getting a small apartment on First Avenue. The city's rapid pace was a perfect fit for Tony's curious and fast-moving mind. 'It was a big deal for him to just go to New York and do what he did,' remembers Russo, 'he was brave.' After a brief flirtation with photography, Viramontez (as he spelled his name at the time) attended the Fashion Institute of Technology (FIT), then alternated between classes at Parsons School of Design and the School of Visual Arts (SVA). The next few years were extremely productive for Tony and he made many of the friends with whom he would later team up in professional life.

Through René Russo he met make-up artist Way Bandy, from whom his diary notes he was to learn a lot about 'style and sophistication'. Bandy in turn introduced him to model Tina Chow, who had already established herself as one of Antonio Lopez's house models. Chow forged the link between Tony and his boyhood hero Lopez, who was then at the height of his fame as a fashion illustrator.

Lopez took a shine to Viramontes and acted as a mentor, offering advice, recommendations and the occasional job, and inviting him to parties. He also advised him to study with his former tutor Jack Potter. Lopez always advised aspiring artists to study with Potter. Potter's class 'Drawing and Thinking' had become a staple at SVA where he was to teach for some 45 years.

'This was a no-nonsense class,' remembers illustrator Bil Donovan. 'It was Jack's movie and he was the star attraction.' Potter, who had been a friend of Carl Erickson (known as Eric) and championed the work of the Renés Bouché and Gruau, had a dictum that the lines his students drew should not be 'sorta, kinda, maybe' but 'straight! curved! fluid!' He maintained that once you walked into room 502 you were in his world. 'But it was not the modern world,' remembers Chuck Nitzberg, a contemporary and classmate of Viramontes. Potter's class was a throwback to his 1950s heyday, when he himself had received coveted commissions from Pond's, *Cosmopolitan* and Coca-Cola. He perpetuated the old-guard, upper-crust, WASP style of drawing in which he himself had been trained. The models were stiff and the poses dated. Daniel Zalkus, another classmate, recalls that 'Sometimes he'd have his models pose by

themselves but usually he'd put them in some sort of scene. Maybe two models at a table watching television, or a few models set up to look like a murder scene.' It was not a come-draw-a-pretty-model class, acknowledges Donovan: 'It was a thinking class, you were challenged to think before you drew.' Donovan remembers that while most of the students in the class were still formalizing their style, 'Tony already seemed ahead of the pack and was in touch with what was or wasn't right for his vision.'

He stayed only a few semesters. But for the first time he had a major artistic breakthrough. Tony's work had been precise, reflecting the type of drawing he had done at high school, but as he began to trust his own instincts his style became less literal. 'I'm really trying to see and not stylize so much,' he wrote in his diary, 'to really look before I draw; my work is fine but has the potential to be very good. Almost great, but I've got to work. To draw, to paint, to just constantly move my hand and draw.'

More to his liking and certainly more influential on both his personal and artistic development were Steven Meisel's classes at Parsons. Meisel, who had worn only black since leaving high school, cut an impressive and enigmatic figure. Though only two years older than Tony, he had already begun to make his mark as an illustrator at *Women's Wear Daily*, where he worked alongside veteran fashion artist Kenneth Paul Block. To boost his meagre earnings Meisel taught a drawing class two nights a week at Parsons, where he himself had studied. 'Steven's classes were exhilarating,' remembers Nitzberg. He was the polar opposite of Jack Potter. 'He allowed you to see how wonderful fashion could be. He made you feel it.' Meisel (a self-confessed 'fashion asshole' since childhood and today a renowned photographer) was one of the few teachers who combined an understanding of the 'old' fashion championed by Potter with the know-how to translate it into 'now' fashion.

The models Meisel used in his classes were either friends – such as Lisa Rosen, Teri Toye and Stephen Sprouse – or other students. There were none of the usual art-school models, who were older and had been around for years. He would style them himself, often playing with gender, putting a girl in a suit and tie, or a man in a wig and heels; 'they always looked chic or kinda crazy', says Nitzberg. The poses were fun, quirky and exaggerated. Meisel encouraged extreme viewpoints. Sometimes Steven himself would pose. Throughout the class he would blast the radio. More than once some other teacher from down the hall at Parsons would come in and complain about the loud music. Tables were set up in a circle with the model in the centre and while the class drew Meisel would race around the room shouting, 'Fuck it up! Hurry! The model is coming down the runway and you have to get it!' He created a real sense of urgency and a charged energy in the room, remembers Nitzberg. 'Sometimes Steven would come from behind, grab you and shake you by the shoulders and scream, "That's it! Give me more!" If he liked what you were doing he would grab the drawing before you were done and pin it to the wall for everyone to see. The goal of each student was to get on that wall. Tony's drawings were almost always on the wall.'

Meisel's class was the catalyst for Tony to refine his craft and cut to the chase. He developed a much looser style of working. His line became a little more trenchant as an early painterly style, albeit a strikingly contemporary one, gave way to simple outlines and minimal marks. 'Steven made me loosen up,' wrote Tony. 'I was seeing a lot of Kenneth Paul Block's work in *Women's Wear Daily*, and it was a faster, much easier style for me to work in. A little bit looser, slightly imperfect. Finished but not polished, or polished but not finished.'

The two inspired each other creatively and shared a strong conspiratorial streak. Together, many found them a little scary: 'There was just so much attitude there,' remembers Donovan, 'they seemed to feed off one another, gossip and innuendo at the sake of someone else to get a laugh.' Through Meisel, Tony's presence became more visible. Steven was his passport to the inner circle of Manhattan's demi-monde with all its social hierarchies and cliquishness. Evenings were spent in the pursuit of fabulousness amongst the denizens of the Mudd Club or on the dancefloor at Studio 54. 'We were always looking for new recruits,' remembers model Teri Toye. 'Tony was fun and enthusiastic about fashion.'

The downtown dress-code demanded humour and ingenuity; sartorial radicalism of any kind was encouraged. The clean-cut appearance Tony had favoured when he began taking classes at Parsons, button-down shirts and blue jeans, gave way as he spent more time with Meisel. He developed the look that would last the rest of his life, dressing almost exclusively in black – from the polish on his fingernails to the dirndl skirts over his jeans. 'He had a very particular look,' remembers musician Nick Rhodes, 'but people did then.' It was all very Spanish, recalls jeweller BillyBoy*. 'I can still see him throwing his shawl over his shoulder like he was about to do a flamenco. He had this beautiful, heavy black hair, thick like a horse's mane, and was made up with very exaggerated eyebrows.'

After graduation, Viramontes remained in New York, where he caught the attention of the Japanese couturier Hanae Mori. Madame Mori, the first Asian woman to be admitted as a member of Chambre Syndicale de la Haute Couture, was impressed by the simplicity and originality of Tony's work. 'The power of his brushstroke was so strong it caught me immediately,' she recalls. 'It was not yet matured, but for one so young he was extremely sensitive to trends. Tony came to my studio to show me his portfolio, and although he seemed shy, his ability to express himself in a minimal style shone through.' Mori offered Viramontes some work and advised him to go to Paris, where she herself had an atelier.

He hung on in New York, doing small ad campaigns for Mori, Bergdorf Goodman and Calvin Klein Cosmetics. But as his profile began to rise, Tony's problems multiplied. Often his drawings were discarded or changes were requested. 'He was ahead of his time, and that scared people,' says hairdresser Bob Recine. Even when his drawings did run, he grew increasingly upset about the way they were used. In 1982 he took Mori's advice and, like so many fashion illustrators before him, left for Paris. 'At that point in time a place like New York was still very conservative compared to Paris,' remembers Recine. 'Anyone at that time who wanted to explore the norms of our business and go beyond it had to go to Paris.'

Settling in a small studio on the Place de la Contrescarpe, Viramontes began making the rounds of the city's agencies and design houses. Tony spoke no French and had difficulty finding his way around. His portfolio was promising but incomplete. It was an inauspicious start. Eugenia Melian, an assistant at Dominique Peclers, remembers a diminutive, black-swathed Viramontes arriving at the offices of the forecast house looking for work. 'I was very junior but had been called in to translate,' she recalls. 'When I saw his book I slipped my number under the table. I remember saying to him "Don't even think about coming to work here".' Melian felt the company would overwork and exploit him, leaving little time for him to complete his portfolio.

Eugenia met up with Tony later that evening and offered to help him navigate the city, becoming the first of his three French agents (the others were Catherine Mathis and Marion de Beaupre). Fresh from a series of internships with some of the city's leading fashion houses, Melian hit the 'phones, calling all the people she had met. 'I called Lucinda Chambers at British *Vogue*, we were old schoolfriends; I called Jean Pierre Joly at Woolmark – they sponsored a lot of the designers' shows; anyone who might be able to open a door.' Melian also helped Viramontes complete his portfolio, calling fashion houses to borrow clothes and herself modelling for Tony. 'I would sit in his tiny apartment posing for him,' she recalls. 'He shaved my hair off, gave me a Mohawk. I would be there from 7pm until 2am posing. I was just wheeling and dealing, calling as many people as I could.'

Paris agreed with Tony and commissions from *Marie Claire* and Prosper Assouline's entirely illustrated *La Mode en Peinture* quickly came his way. In 1983 he traded his small studio in the fifth arrondisement for a grand third-floor apartment in the fashionable seventh at Avenue de Saxe. It was a typical nineteenth-century space that occupied an entire floor and had three enormous fireplaces. The apartment was 'incredible', remembers close friend Sophie de Taillac. 'It was totally white. There wasn't much furniture, a salon with a drawing table, some bedrooms and a kitchen. It was him: black in a white space. I could ring the doorbell at any time and he would always be up.'

Tony's new studio quickly became every bit as chaotic as Warhol's infamous Factory. He was looking to test boundaries creatively and he soon gathered a pool of young model–muses and like-minded creatives capable of making the journey with him. Amongst the assemblage were Bob Recine, make-up artist Paul Gobal, stylist Frédérique Lorca and studio manager Susann Güenther. This was to be the beginning of Tony's career-long practice of hiring and surrounding himself with friends, seamlessly blending his personal and professional lives. While there was something a little insular about Tony's crowd, it was this gang-like mentality that underpinned their creative energy.

'It was a kind of 1980s Factory in the middle of this very bourgeois area of Paris,' remembers Lorca. 'People passed through in droves, models would call by on go-sees, Tony would draw them, snap Polaroids and make them over.' Such creative disorganization, while being inspiring, proved difficult to manage, though Viramontes thrived on the chaos. 'The 'phone rang non-stop,' recalls Güenther, and the neighbours complained about the noise. 'It was usually the music,' remembers Eugenia Melian, 'opera or something by Philip Glass … Tony loved the high notes. "Imagine you're an opera singer," he would tell his models, "try and hit that high note".'

Tony would often start drawing late in the afternoon, remembers Güenther, and continue until four or five in the morning. 'The threat of a deadline stimulated him into a kind of desperate creativity,' she recalls. 'It was remarkable to observe his composure as he sketched. He seemed to create extemporaneously, almost without any effort. He was so agile, it came so easily to him, it didn't seem like a struggle, there were no grunts and groans, papers crumpled-up with anguish. Everything was so fluid.'

While Tony was purposeful in his work he applied an equal measure of concentrated energy to his social life, which he led at a similar pace. He was a regular at Le Sept and Le Palace on Rue du Faubourg Montmartre, a legendary establishment created by Fabrice Emaer along the lines of New York's Studio 54 and a focal-point of gossipy Parisian nightlife. Viramontes was always the centre of attention, recalls Surrealist jewellery designer BillyBoy* (of BillyBoy* & Lala): 'He could be terribly amusing and told anecdotes about the great and glamorous with enormous aplomb.' Together with his best friend of the moment Princess Gloria von Thurn und Taxis he was out all night, every night, exploring the capital's most avant-garde nightspots, where fashion was being created. 'We were like Alice in Wonderland,' recalls the dynamic Princess famed for her vertiginous hairdos. 'Everything was there, a little bit too big for us because we were so young, but we thought we can still taste and enjoy it.' Never off-duty, Tony would get a lot of jobs through his nocturnal adventures. 'Paris was very villagey at the time,' recalls Melian, 'everyone knew each other and artists spoke to each other more directly back then.'

Melian's telephone campaigns were also begining to pay off as British *Vogue* commissioned Viramontes to create a series of drawings celebrating 'the new femme fatale' for the December 1983 issue of the magazine. 'I was astounded by his work,' remembers fashion editor Lucinda Chambers, 'it was so fully formed and effort-less.' After persuading the magazine's editor, Beatrix Miller, to commission Viramontes, Chambers set off for Paris with dozens of hats and milliner Stephen Jones in tow. Jones, just beginning his ascent in the world of high fashion, remembers being very impressed by Tony's fashionable Parisian address and the excitement of seeing the dynamic world of *Vogue* in action: tense 'phonecalls to New York, vintage champagne, extravagant creativity, a tantrum or two and all before 11am. Tony insisted on working from life and he wanted the

models in full hair and make-up and dressed correctly. Then he would start drawing. He was also very specific about the kind of model he wanted. He liked noses. He didn't want "pretty" girls. He thought pretty girls couldn't wear hats. … He must have produced a hundred drawings that day; I remember the pile kept getting higher. Each one took about ten minutes, five, sometimes less. Leslie Winer was the model [in Jones's hats] and when he was happy with a pose he would shout, "Hold that!" And he kept talking the whole time.'

The moment he began drawing Tony became totally locked in. He could draw for hours, energetically and with command. Melian remembers that he once got so excited by what he was doing that he 'cut the end off his finger [while sharpening his pencil with a blade] – blood everywhere and he still didn't stop'. Life ran at a hot pace for Tony that year. His international reputation quickly grew as he proved he could handle editorial, advertising and portraiture commissions with equal ease and in June 1983 Viramontes made the first of many trips to Tokyo. At the behest of Hanae Mori, the graphic designer Ikko Tanaka, creative director of 'The Best Five' show, extended an invitation to Tony to create the promotional artwork for Japan's annual runway show celebrating the work of five internationally renowned designers; 1984 saw Vivienne Westwood, Calvin Klein,

ABOVE: **'THE BEST FIVE'** IN TOKYO TONY'S DRAWINGS FOR 'THE BEST FIVE' SHOW BECAME A POWERFUL INFLUENCE ON A NEW GENERATION OF DESIGN AND GRAPHICS STUDENTS. JAPAN, 1984

OPPOSITE:
MADAME BUTTERFLY A PASTEL PROFILE OF MADAME HANAE MORI, TONY'S FIRST PATRON AND GREATEST CHEERLEADER. WHEN ASKED BY AN AMERICAN JOURNALIST WHERE SHE DISCOVERED VIRAMONTES, MME. MORI REPLIED 'WHY, IN YOUR OWN BACKYARD'. JAPAN, 1984. COLLECTION OF HANAE MORI, COURTESY OF THE HANAE MORI FOUNDATION

Gianfranco Ferré, Claude Montana and Hanae Mori honoured. 'Tokyo suits me well, compared to New York, Paris, or London this city is just overflowing with energy,' Viramontes reflected.

While Tony's work in London had previously been confined to the high-fashion pages of glossy Condé Nast titles including *Vogue* and *Tatler*, a blossoming friendship with Ray Petri opened new doors in the capital. Petri was a stylist long before it became a coveted job description and was at the epicentre of British street style. He mixed classic high-end pieces with streetwear in a natural but haphazard manner at a time when fashion was all about shoulder pads and power dressing. Working with a small group of friends Petri founded the Buffalo label and provided the effortless mix of looks that characterized the early editions of *i-D* and *The Face*. Tony became a peripheral member of the Buffalo crew through his relationship with Petri and began to draw heavily on the group's ideology for inspiration, often sketching impromptu at Petri's shoots with photographer Jamie Morgan, taking advantage of the set-up of models and styling. Petri encouraged Viramontes to explore a new agenda outside the fashion system and became an important source of work for Tony in London.

After an introduction by Petri, jewellery designer Nicky Butler asked Viramontes to create two billboards for the windows of his store on London's Fulham Road. He remembers how the work unfolded before his very eyes. 'I wanted something to tie in with the 1984 Olympic Games, like a strong Leni Riefenstahl image. Tony basically drew Ray, who had the most beautiful chiselled face, and added in some earrings. The music was on and wonderful drawings came, then Tony said we should carry this [theme] throughout the store, so he did a bunch of smaller drawings which I then stuck jewellery on and he put them in the windows in frames.' Further commissions followed and Tony sketched for Boots cosmetics, womenswear label Joseph and Browns' South Molton Street store.

In 1984 Melian relocated to Italy 'where everything was happening' and began to show Tony's portfolio to Milan's leading creatives. After seeing his book, Maggie Newman at Audience thought that Tony might be a good fit for the Genius Group, a think tank led by Adriano Goldschmied that created a number of rather disparate labels including Diesel, Goldie, Replay, Bobo Kaminsky, Martin Guy and Ten Big Boys. Goldschmied wanted to create a unified global brand and decided Tony would be the perfect person to do it. This marked a bold new phase in Viramontes's work as he picked up a camera for the first time since high school. The large-format Polaroid became Tony's tool of choice. He would complete his prints by adding animated, striking sweeps of colour using collage and paint pens.

Tony's photographic work shares many of the characteristics of his drawings. He may have changed his medium but the end result was the same. 'He made powerful shapes and forms,' says Barry Kamen, who suggests that photography offered Viramontes some creative privacy. 'The eyes upon him when he was drawing, it seemed too much to bear.' More and more, the artist in Viramontes

bridled at the conventions of fashion. When writer Nicholas Drake came calling in late 1984, Viramontes was keen to shake off the label and associations of the commercial artist, insisting that he was an artistic creator, a creator of ideas in images. 'I'm sort of in a transitional period in my life,' he said. 'I don't want to be doing what I'm doing forever. Illustration is a bridge, a crossing to lead me to other areas. I also want to get into video.' Restless and dissatisfied, Viramontes needed continual stimulation: 'I look for new ideas because I always want to be in a state of creative anxiety and insecurity. If I feel sure of myself I cannot be creative. I try to renew myself.' To that end, he began to experiment more heavily with drugs. 'Tony wanted to see colours in a spectrum not usually in a mind,' suggests Bob Recine. 'He was looking for something beyond himself and he viewed drugs as a new street to walk, not on the map.' Heroin quickly became his drug of choice. 'I think cocaine was too bright for him. I think he wanted to be overpowered, as he was such a powerful person[ality]. Heroin would bring him to his knees.'

Recine felt that Tony's creativity stemmed from his exploration of himself through his use of drugs. 'He had a very uncanny natural instinct towards fashion, he just knew his take on things was very individual, very engaging. Tony never really looked at magazines, he always looked at the past and personalities, it just never seemed to regurgitate itself in a way that you would realize where it had come from.' Recine suggests that Tony actually prefigured the birth of heroin chic 'in the sense it was not a look. Tony was a heroin addict; he recreated what was around him. It was not anything other than the realness of the moment: boys in make-up; Tony was wearing make-up. Boys with hats and headscarves; Tony was wearing those kinds of things.' Viramontes created his own images of the times, following fashion where it corresponded with his own intentions. 'It might sound mysterious,' he said, 'but what I paint in my work is simply my own image. I want to bring out and express a mood. I want to convey my inner world through a medium controlled by my own hand.' Viramontes saw himself as both the medium and the message.

As Eugenia Melian remembers, 'Tony's drug habit quickly went from being very private and contained to public and all-consuming … He began to burn a lot of bridges in Paris; he did not behave very well.' Cyril Brulé noticed that 'He became a bit of a diva, arriving late, asking for the impossible, being super difficult.' But he was still artistic enough to be respected despite the hysteria and hang-ups. Bob Recine recalls, 'When Tony was at his peak he was the toast of Paris, he was creating a new road. People recognized and respected that. The drug addiction and the dramas were part of that and were accepted because it was something new. Frequently, insecure clients hired him because he had an eye and the buzz, but Tony had his own set of rules and if you wanted him, you had to play by those rules.' If you wanted input from Tony but did not understand him you were in for a rough ride, says Recine. Tony did not want a job, he did not want to follow, he wanted to create. Cyril Brulé recalls that Viramontes 'would go to a meeting at an advertising agency or with an art

director and they would give him a brief and explain what they wanted and he would say, "Forget it, your idea is shit, this is what I can do for you".'

Tony became adept at getting his own way when it came to dealing with art directors and clients alike. 'When he realized he was not going to get his way, his calling card was to create absolute destruction,' says Recine, 'to make that person pay for their inanity – to actually realize what they were looking at.'

He would get angry and not in the kind of way that you would imagine a man who would wear make-up would act. Tony was a very masculine figure in the sense of taking command, he could be quite the swashbuckler. If people did not understand or approve of his work then he would inflame and exaggerate it even more. His aim was to make people understand that what they can see now they will understand later. For a lot of people it was to be the first and last time. But for others such as Claude Montana and Hanae Mori, who gave him incredible freedom, he produced some of his most memorable work.

Tony's relationship with the imperialistic Mori was 'the absolute perfect marriage', remembers Bob Recine. 'She treated him like a son, and gave him the freedom to say what he wanted to say. There were no guidelines; she saw the immense talent that he had as an illustrator and harnessed it. At that time no one could touch Tony, there were a few people out there trying new creative directions but nobody who would actually explode

things in your face in the way he did.' Gradually his role evolved so that Viramontes not only created illustrations for the house but also assisted Mori anonymously in the creation of her haute couture collections. For while Mori felt it important that she appear publicly to be the sole creator of her designs, she relied on a small team of sketch artists to generate ideas for the hundreds of gowns she produced each year. Tony joined Randal Meyers at Madame's Paris atelier and together they sketched, side by side, updating the chiffon dresses that fluttered gracefully with her signature butterfly prints. 'Mori was always very respectful of Tony and creative people in general,' remembers Meyers. 'She would talk to us individually, going over our croquis, and chose from the options we provided what she felt worked best for her. If Tony knew that you respected him, you could not meet a more charming and cooperative person.' 'I can't think of anyone to whom he gave more respect than Hanae Mori,' says Recine. 'He would bend his own rules for her'.

Similarly, Claude Montana allowed Viramontes an unprecedented level of creative freedom. 'I would let him do what he felt like doing,' remembers Montana, 'he was an artist. I would sometimes show him a sketch of mine so that he would have an idea of my collection's silhouette, or give him an indication of colour. A presentation at that time might have between ten and 15 groups of colours. He would pick one out of them and do a sketch. He was very easy-going and very fast.' Montana's fashion shows were amongst the first to excel in styling and presentation. The invitations Viramontes

ABOVE: **TINA CHOW**
THE RENOWNED
CLOTHESHORSE TINA CHOW
PROVIDED VIRAMONTES
WITH HIS FIRST GLIMPSE OF
THE FASHIONABLE WORLD
OF HAUTE COUTURE.
POLAROIDS BY VIRAMONTES.
NEW YORK, c. 1982

OPPOSITE:
LISABETH GARBER
NEVER INTERESTED IN
THE GIRL NEXT DOOR,
VIRAMONTES ADORED
MODEL LISABETH GARBER.
IN THIS UNFINISHED
PORTRAIT SKETCH HE
GRAPPLES WITH HER
PROFILE, UNABLE TO LAY
DOWN HER NOSE TO HIS
SATISFACTION. ROME, 1984

designed for his annual presentations quickly became collectors' items and the hottest tickets in town.

By 1984 the fashion world had well and truly caught on and Viramontes attained a fashion nirvana when, after an introduction by fashion editor Franca Sozzani, he was summoned to Rome by the couturier Valentino Garavani to create a portfolio of drawings that were to mark his silver jubilee celebrations in the pages of *Vogue Italia*. Sozzani recalls that 'while people have always perceived Valentino to be very classical, Giancarlo Giammetti [the couturier's business partner] was always looking for young and avant-garde people to work with' to keep the brand current and relevant. 'Haute couture at the time was perceived to be rather staid,' remembers Tony's agent Eugenia Melian. But he was able to give Garavani's ruffles a new twist: 'Viramontes made Valentino very modern,' says Giammetti, 'and that was very important. I thought that fashion illustrated by an artist would be very eye-catching and new. It evokes a dream, we sell dreams and romance [and] Tony knew how to do it with a few strokes.' The intricacies of Valentino's gowns inspired Viramontes to create some of his most defiantly high-fashion images. 'The clothes were so complex to draw, it was almost like an exercise,' remembers model Lisabeth Garber. 'Tony's sketches were intuitive, right out of the hand.' 'He was quite free,' concurs Giammetti, 'he worked very quickly and if something did not work for me, he would redo it immediately.'

Tony's previously undernourished palette flared into a kaleidoscope of colours during the commission and the Viramontes woman really came into her own. Garber's sidelong glances became more alluring than ever before, her lips redder, the thrust of her shoulders more abandoned. Tony's razor-like lines evoked a bold, powerful woman. 'Tony really knew how to capture the world of the people he was working for,' says Cyril Brulé.

Tony's work with Valentino caught the attention of musician Nick Rhodes, one fifth of pop group Duran Duran. The group was one of the most successful bands of the 1980s and a leading proponent of the new MTV age in which image was rapidly becoming as important as the music itself. In the midst of their Duran Duran obligations, Simon Le Bon, Nick Rhodes and Roger Taylor took some time out to 'rediscover their musical inspiration' and formed Arcadia, an experimental splinter group. Arcadia produced one album, 'So Red The Rose', filled with moody tunes and an ambient, intricate blend of the avant-garde. Nick Rhodes drafted in Viramontes to create the album's sleeve art and capture the group's aesthetic. Rhodes had been introduced to Tony in Paris by model Violeta Sanchez, and loved his style. 'I thought that Tony was a newer, edgier version of Antonio [Lopez],' he recalls. Historically it had always been Rhodes who had led the way when it came to mapping out the group's visuals and he felt that for this particular album an artwork would be preferable to a photograph. 'It just seemed to be the right feeling for the album to have something free-flowing and beautiful.'

Rhodes recalls that it was Tony's suggestion they use Sanchez for the record sleeve. 'They had worked together previously and had a great relationship, we all loved Violeta's fabulous profile. She is one of those exquisite creatures that look beautiful from every direction. Her deportment was second to none, she knew just how to position her arms and move her body to create the right shapes. Once we decided upon Violeta we really just let Tony play around.' The sittings for the paintings took place some months later in New York at the Andrée Putman-designed Morgans Hotel on Madison Avenue. For Tony, who had always viewed his success in Paris as a stepping-stone to returning triumphant to New York, the commission was a coup.

Viramontes 'knew exactly what he was after, and changed the styling constantly; he tied up her hair in scarves, then came the big earrings, the red lips and fingernails. He was determined to get it right; he did painting after painting after painting,' recounts Rhodes. Sanchez recalls that Viramontes drew for 'close to 12 hours a day for almost a week. It was hard work, when

'Violeta had an elegance to her, an old style classic beauty.'

NICK RHODES

you found the pose that he liked you had to stay still.'
Tony was initally nervous and demanding as he worked,
until he got to the point where he felt he was getting
what he wanted; then he would get excited. Tony had a
fluid stroke and was so quick that he would create each
painting in a matter of minutes.

Rhodes remembers that Viramontes was a little more
reticent when it came to creating portraits of the group.
'I think Tony was definitely more comfortable drawing
women. With Violeta he was swishing his arms around
and cocking his hat, really creating one sketch after
another. With us the process was a little more laboured,
he was more concerned about likeness, that it wasn't
quite right or he needed to get our features spot-on but
I said to him, "Look it's an interpretation. We're looking
for a really beautiful interpretation".' The record sleeve
of 'So Red The Rose' perfectly describes the mood of the
record within. After going Platinum, Arcadia faded to a
footnote in 1980s pop, as Le Bon, Rhodes and Taylor
resumed work with Duran Duran on 'Notorious' in 1986.

Tony's frenetic pace gradually began to take its toll as
he continued to travel between London, Paris, Rome
and Japan. He began losing his hair. 'It was coming out
in handfuls,' remembers Eugenia Melian, who arranged
for him to see a doctor. 'He was told to slow down, that
he had been putting himself under a lot of pressure and
was suffering from stress.' But his symptoms showed
little sign of abating and by the end of 1986 Viramontes
had been diagnosed with HIV and was seriously ill.
This was the decade when sex turned deadly, as did the
drugs that fuelled the revelry. The party that had begun
so effortlessly lost its energy and the hangover kicked in.
'Tony became anxious and scared when he got sick,'
remembers Brulé. The only person he told about his
condition was his older brother Ed. 'As close as I was to
Tony,' recalls Recine, 'he never said "I have AIDS", it
was a kind of silent understanding.'

VIOLETA SANCHEZ
THIS PREVIOUSLY
UNPUBLISHED SLEEVE
ART FOR ARCADIA'S
'SO RED THE ROSE'
HAS A LYRICAL
EXTRAVAGANCE.
NEW YORK, 1985.
COLLECTION
OF NICK RHODES

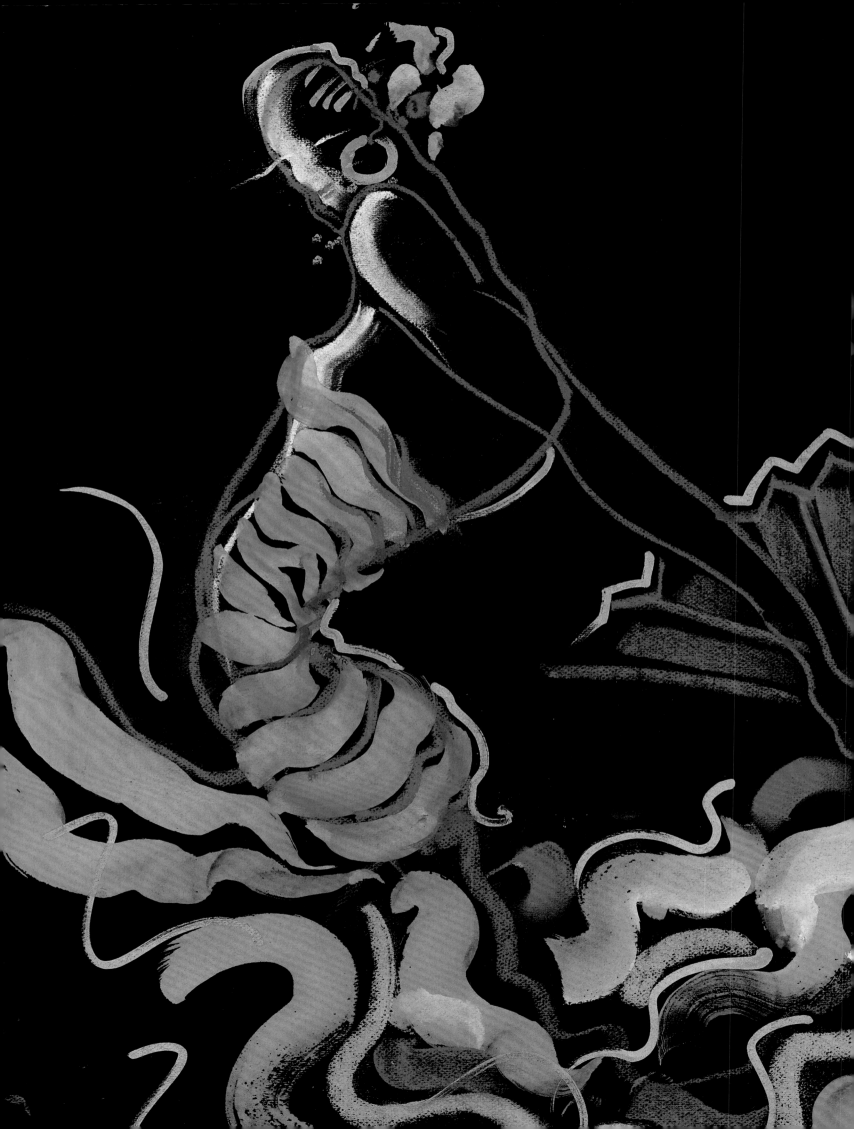

After completing a campaign for the cosmetics company
Rochas and a cover story with Nina Hagen for German
Vogue, Viramontes left Paris and returned to his family
home in Los Angeles, where he worked sporadically,
creating the sleeve art for Janet Jackson's groundbreaking album 'Control' and a few smaller projects with Sly
Fox, The Motels and Donna Summer. His condition had
rendered him unreliable for extended periods and
gradually his work appeared with increasing irregular-
ity. 'When I would see him in Los Angeles in those later
days he was fragile,' recalls Bob Recine. 'I think that
Tony felt a bit useless without the chaos of his life in
Paris. That chaos gave him something in his work – he
needed that intensity to be Viramontes, without it he felt
a little unimportant. So he chose to stop working, rather
than continue in a state of mind that made him feel that
he did not really have that much to say.'

In 1987, as his condition deteriorated, Viramontes
looked back on his short but eventful career as he
began collaboration with the Japanese publisher Ryuko
Tsushin on a dazzling monograph dedicated to his work.
In February 1988 Tony made what would be his final
trip to Japan, to attend the opening of an exhibition
sponsored by Hanae Mori that was to coincide with the
publication of his book.

Tony Viramontes died of AIDS just three months later,
on 23 May 1988. He was 31. For all too brief a period
Viramontes became the voice of fashion, or at least its
timekeeper. After a small funeral attended by his
immediate family he was interred in a mausoleum at
Holy Cross Cemetery in Culver City. Barry Kamen
believes that had he lived, Tony's love of drawing
would have prevailed over the mixed media work he
was doing shortly before his death: 'He had a natural
talent, something special and rare. He could articulate
with his drawings.' While it is tragic that Tony's life
ended with the same speed at which he worked, more
than two decades after his death the magic of his art
has not faded with time, and those achingly effortless
marks, each stroke dead-on perfection, are a lasting
testament to a career whose memory should always be
in the ascendant.

FAN DANCE
VIOLETA SANCHEZ
FOR ARCADIA'S
'SO RED THE ROSE'.
NEW YORK, 1985.
COLLECTION
OF NICK RHODES

ON FASHION

'Draw it, paint it,
love it, understand it.'

VIRAMONTES

Fashion, art and life were indistinguishable to Viramontes.
His aesthetic went far beyond his drawings and he became
a great commercial fashion illustrator. His work captured
movement in fleeting moments – the way a woman might
throw her coat over her shoulders, hold a cigarette or cross
her legs – small gestures that can make clothes and the
women wearing them all the more memorable.

The role of the fashion artist is to sell clothes, to tell the story of a hat or dress, to translate the essence of a garment or accessory into an image of desire. The magazines and designers who commission illustrations demand a clear, unequivocal record of the subject to prevent any queries arising in the minds of their readers; but a fashion illustration must also be evocative. Tony's work successfully conveyed both the detail of the clothing itself and the emotion evoked in a posture. His spontaneous line gave even the most pedestrian clothes a sense of elegance and vitality. Viramontes knew how to accentuate the best features in clothes, condensing garments into a succinct visual shorthand. By instinctively trimming away excess detail, Viramontes captured the memory of a texture; frequently he overlaid one motif with another, rummaged around and pushed out a shape seemingly at random that summoned up the attitude and mood of the clothed figure, while transforming what he saw into something of his own. Fashion was a language and Viramontes quickly developed a feel for the syntax and vocabulary.

Tony's first fashion drawings appeared in *The New York Times* in the late 1970s and were a little on the conservative side. The softly modelled illustrations for Revlon Furs and Charivari exhibit little of the drama of his later work and strongly reflect the influence of Antonio Lopez and Michael Vollbracht, from whom he respectfully took his cues at the time. But gradually, as he gained more confidence and developed his own artistic vocabulary, Tony's style became less referential. 'I need to go beyond what I was doing,' he wrote in his diary. 'I need to look deeper to bring my work to a point where I can establish a style of my own, something more intriguing, more interesting, dramatic and with great feeling.' To that end Viramontes began to sample a wider range of influences, both high and low, going beyond references to contemporary fashion artists. After a nod to the Expressionist painter Egon Schiele, Viramontes flirted lightly with Man Ray and Jean Cocteau, before developing a fascination for drag queens. Throughout his career Viramontes was drawn to the flamboyant subculture of drag and this interest found a wide range of expression in his fashion drawings. 'Drag queens have such attitude,' he said, 'they exploit everything that a woman has that they wish they could have.'

In 1983 Viramontes began to draw Parisian haute couture, then at an apex of opulence and the source of some of the world's most dramatic and splashy high fashion. He embraced it gluttonously. The flamboyance of the moment was a perfect fit for his vocation: fashion swung his way as the hard outlines, bold colours and overt glamour all lent themselves to his pen and paintbrush. Viramontes reported on each season's collections with wit and originality, rapidly amassing the kind of distinguished editorial commissions more frequently earmarked for photographers. From *Le Monde* and *Marie Claire* in France to *Vogue* and *Per Lei* in Italy to *The Face* and *i-D* in London, his work soon populated the pages of all the best fashion publications. Indeed, several glossy tomes described Viramontes as the new saviour of fashion illustration. 'He was an unusual illustrator,' remembers editor Franca Sozzani, 'he had a very strong hand. At a time when photography

dominated the fashion pages, it is difficult to imagine the power that an artist could have in the interpretation of the mood of the moment.'

Viramontes reinvigorated this traditional way of selling fashion through drawing. He reminded people of what the hand had been able to achieve before it was sidelined by the eye of photography. Pioneering new directions to shake up the viewer, Tony developed his style continuously and he became a master of diverse drawing techniques and media: pencil, charcoal, ink, gouache and collage. Occasionally he even used lipsticks, eyebrow pencils and other cosmetics in place of crayons. Tony's drawings were successful because they were completely contemporary. Just when the realism of photography seemed to have triumphed over drawing, Viramontes – with lines as lean as his elongated models – succeeded in bringing fashion illustration back to the fore.

Illustration and photography have both told the story of fashion, but not in the same way. Photography, even at its most ethereal, is mostly treated as fact; fashion illustration as a wish. Tony Viramontes produced fashion drawings that emphatically transcend mere documentary. He painted the mood and spirit of the day with a drive no photograph could match. 'It is a pity, but today there are no more fashion illustrators,' lamented couturier Yves Saint Laurent in 2007. 'For however much I admire photographers, I have to admit that their work is done to the detriment of the design. … In the case of an illustration … the design is well and truly present and alive.' The singular attitude and style that emerged in Tony's fashion drawings was impossible to ignore and impossible to duplicate. It would make him as influential a fashion illustrator as any from the preceding generations. Just as René Gruau's work reflects the confidence and elegance of the upper classes in the 1940s and 1950s, Viramontes's images perfectly capture the younger fashionable woman of the 1980s.

CHANEL

From the moment he arrived at Chanel in 1983, Karl Lagerfeld began to revive the venerable old couture house whose name had faded to signify fine fragrance alone. Ten years after Mademoiselle's death Lagerfeld resurrected Chanel the brand and reinvented it for a new generation, reworking Coco's characteristic designs – still recognizably Chanel, but with a wink. The woollen bouclé suit's hemline rose to expose the knee, appealing to a younger, hipper market at a stroke, and the monogram of interlocking Cs became once again a sought-after membership badge of the fashionable crowd.

PREVIOUS SPREAD:
ROCOCO CHANEL
VIRAMONTES KNEW HOW
TO SUGGEST THE MOOD OF
THE MOMENT; IN THIS
SKETCH OF A SABLE-
TRIMMED EVENING SUIT BY
KARL LARGERFELD FOR
CHANEL HAUTE COUTURE
THERE IS A SENSE OF
WILDFIRE AND OVER-THE-
TOP EIGHTIES STYLE.
PARIS, 1984

OPPOSITE: **HIGH DRAMA**
DRAWN FOR *MADAME
FIGARO*. VIRAMONTES
EXPERTLY COMMANDS THE
PAGE IN THIS TYPICALLY
ASSURED DRAWING OF
CHANEL HAUTE COUTURE.
TRANSPARENT WASHES OF
COLOUR LIFT THE SKETCHY
DRAWING FROM THE PAPER.
PARIS, 1986

CHRISTIAN DIOR
SEAMLESSLY BLENDING THE
CLASSY WITH THE
GLAMOROUS, VIRAMONTES'S
DISTINCTIVE STYLE AND
BOLD COLOUR PALETTE
CREATE A POTENT
HIGH-FASHION COCKTAIL IN
THIS STUDY OF DIOR HAUTE
COUTURE BY MARC BOHAN.
PARIS, 1984

CHRISTIAN DIOR

Following the untimely death of Christian Dior in 1957 and the brief, angst-ridden tenure of Yves Saint Laurent, Marc Bohan took over the direction of Maison Dior in 1960 and remained until 1989. During his first decade at Dior, Bohan gained a reputation as a designer who could turn street style into haute couture, maintaining the elegance of the house without sacrificing the youthful spirit of the clothes.

MISS DIOR
ORIGINALLY DRAWN FOR *LE FIGARO*'S GUIDE TO THE COLLECTIONS, THIS DIOR EVENING DRESS WITH ASYMMETRICAL NECKLINE IS CAPTURED BY VIRAMONTES IN A SERIES OF SWIFT EXPRESSIVE BRUSH STROKES. PARIS, 1986

BLACKGLAMA

Noted more for eye-catching ad campaigns than for the cut of its coats, Blackglama the label was conceived in 1968 by advertising executive Jane Trahey, for the Great Lakes Mink Association (GLMA), which was producing dark furs. The early images were shot by Richard Avedon and featured high-profile filmstars such as Audrey Hepburn and Elizabeth Taylor swathed in Blackglama mink. The memorable tag line, 'What becomes a Legend most?' has topped the iconic full-page black and white print ads for more than four decades.

BLACKGLAMA
'WHAT BECOMES A LEGEND
MOST?' ASKED THE
LONG-RUNNING CAMPAIGN
BY ICONIC FURRIER
BLACKGLAMA. MINK, OF
COURSE! DRAWN FOR
LA MODE EN PEINTURE.
PARIS, 1984

LÉON
VISSOT

Established in postwar Paris, the house of Vissot was
the principal furrier to the city's demi-monde. Maison
Vissot stood at 49, Faubourg St Honoré and dealt in
only the most exotic and luxurious of animal skins.
Cheetah, seal and monkey fur were its stock in
trade. Upon the death of Vissot in 1960
Bernard Perris, who later worked at
Jean-Louis Scherrer, took control of
the house and rejuvenated its fur
designs with his unusual and
unexpected pelt combinations.

LÉON VISSOT
ALL ABOUT TEXTURE, THIS
ILLUSTRATION DRAWS
PARALLELS BETWEEN
THE MODEL'S BRUTALLY
CROPPED HAIR AND THE
TACTILE ASTRAKHAN
FUR OF A MINK-EDGED
ASTRAKHAN SUIT BY LÉON
VISSOT. PARIS, 1984

LADY LUXE
VIRAMONTES WAS NOT
AFRAID OF LADYLIKE CHIC.
IN THIS SKETCH OF
GIVENCHY HAUTE COUTURE
HE MIXES SARTORIAL
RESTRAINT WITH EXUBER-
ANT PATTERNS AND COLOUR.
PARIS, 1984

HUBERT DE GIVENCHY

A master of understated elegance, Givenchy's aesthetic was pure, ladylike classicism with an occasional surprising flourish. The French aristocrat became a household name through his collaborations with actress Audrey Hepburn, dressing her for iconic roles in *Sabrina*, *Breakfast at Tiffany's* and *My Fair Lady*. 'His are the only clothes in which I am myself,' she told reporters in 1956. Givenchy's designs were epitomized by his mastery of the 'little black dress', which he presented in a variety of chic styles and fabrics, from ribbed cotton piqué to Italian satin.

EMMANUEL UNGARO

A protégé of master couturier Balenciaga, Emmanuel Ungaro learned from him a passion for cutting and draping cloth to fit and flatter the body. His designs expressed the beauty in volume without imposing structure or sacrificing comfort; his flowing gowns were at once elegant and seductive. Ungaro collections revealed a confident sense of play with a broad colour spectrum and bold pattern.

VALENTINO

Dubbed the 'Sheik of Chic' by *Women's Wear Daily*, Valentino Garavani loves dresses – his eponymous label Valentino means dresses and has done for nearly 45 years. Bewitched by any form of unabashedly feminine detail, each season he hones his frilly, frothy gowns to the delight of the rich, thin and royal. To mark 25 years' service to his frequently 'best-dressed' clientele, the designer commissioned Viramontes to create a portfolio of commemorative drawings. It was an inspired pairing – Valentino, who had long presented a temple to the pretty, the feminine, the enchanting, and Viramontes, the *enfant terrible* of fashion illustration.

Viramontes relished the superb detailing, the bows and ruffles, the embroideries; effortlessly he draws our attention to the essence of Valentino's extravaganzas, suggesting the texture of a chiffon, the lustre of a bead or the shimmer of a satin, all with an economy of expression that grows increasingly vague until gradually the details disappear. While the drawings push the edge of sex and sexuality they remain very much about elegance and sophistication. 'There was one drawing that I adored,' recalls Lisabeth Garber. 'Tony was trying to get my nose right and hadn't got it right, so I essentially had three noses – but it was awesome.' The sessions took place in Rome at the luxurious Hotel de la Ville where Viramontes managed to run up a room-service bill for almost double the fee he received for creating drawings. 'He was being an absolute brat,' laughs Garber, 'having people run all over the place for every little thing he asked for, but it was very relaxed. I would put on the outfit, do something and he would draw. That's how we worked. Every once in a while he would make a face and ask for something stronger.' Valentino loved the drawings and splashed them across dozens of pages in *Vogue Italia*. 'It validated every-thing,' says Eugenia Melian.

VIVA VALENTINO
VIRAMONTES PRODUCED
SOME OF VALENTINO'S MOST
EVOCATIVE AND
BEAUTIFULLY OBSERVED
ADVERTISING IMAGERY. HIS
ARTICULATE AND
INIMITABLE LINE GAVE THE
COUTURIER'S FRILLY,
FROTHY GOWNS A BOLD AND
CONTEMPORARY NEW TWIST.
ROME, 1984

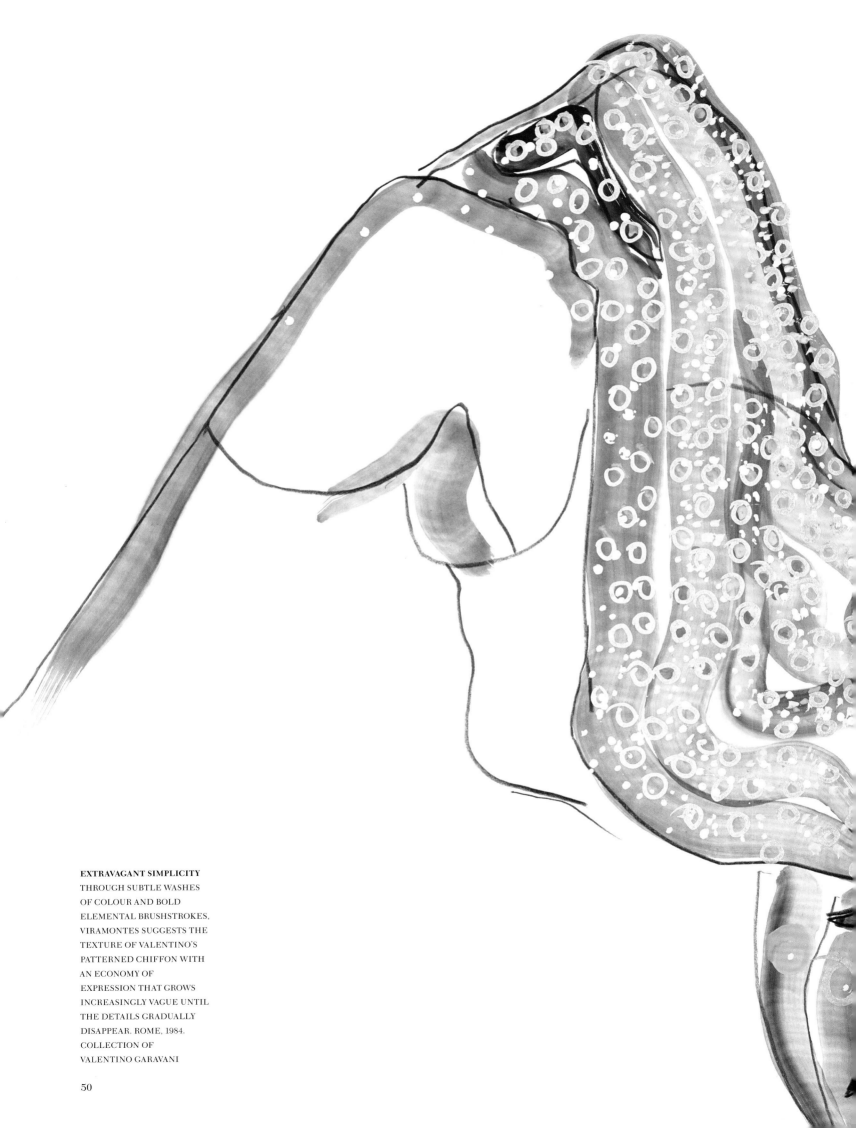

EXTRAVAGANT SIMPLICITY
THROUGH SUBTLE WASHES
OF COLOUR AND BOLD
ELEMENTAL BRUSHSTROKES,
VIRAMONTES SUGGESTS THE
TEXTURE OF VALENTINO'S
PATTERNED CHIFFON WITH
AN ECONOMY OF
EXPRESSION THAT GROWS
INCREASINGLY VAGUE UNTIL
THE DETAILS GRADUALLY
DISAPPEAR. ROME, 1984.
COLLECTION OF
VALENTINO GARAVANI

GLAMAZON
DEFIANTLY GLAMOROUS,
THE VIRAMONTES WOMAN
REALLY CAME INTO HER
OWN IN TONY'S WORK WITH
VALENTINO. HER GLANCE
BECAME MORE ALLURING,
HER LIPS DARKER, THE
THRUST OF HER SHOULDERS
MORE ABANDONED.
ROME, 1984. COLLECTION
OF VALENTINO GARAVANI

MÉNAGE À TROIS
VIRAMONTES LOVED TO
PROVOKE AND KNEW HOW
TO TIP THE BALANCE OF A
DRAWING WITH A SOUPÇON
OF SEX. BUT NO MATTER
HOW OUTRÉ THE FINAL
COMPOSITION, HIS
DRAWINGS ALWAYS HAD
THE SOUND TECHNICAL
UNDERPINNINGS OF A
CONSPICUOUSLY GIFTED
DRAUGHTSMAN AND
RETAIN AN ELEGANCE
AND SOPHISTICATION.
ROME, 1984. COLLECTION
OF VALENTINO GARAVANI

FLOWER POWER
PARTIAL TO THE ODD FRILL
OR FLOWER, VALENTINO
MADE HIS MARK WITH HIS
INTRICATELY DETAILED
AND LUXURIOUS
ENSEMBLES. VIRAMONTES'S
EYE FOR PATTERN IS
BEAUTIFULLY REALIZED IN
THIS CHARACTERISTICALLY
BOLD SKETCH. ROME, 1984.
COLLECTION OF
VALENTINO GARAVANI

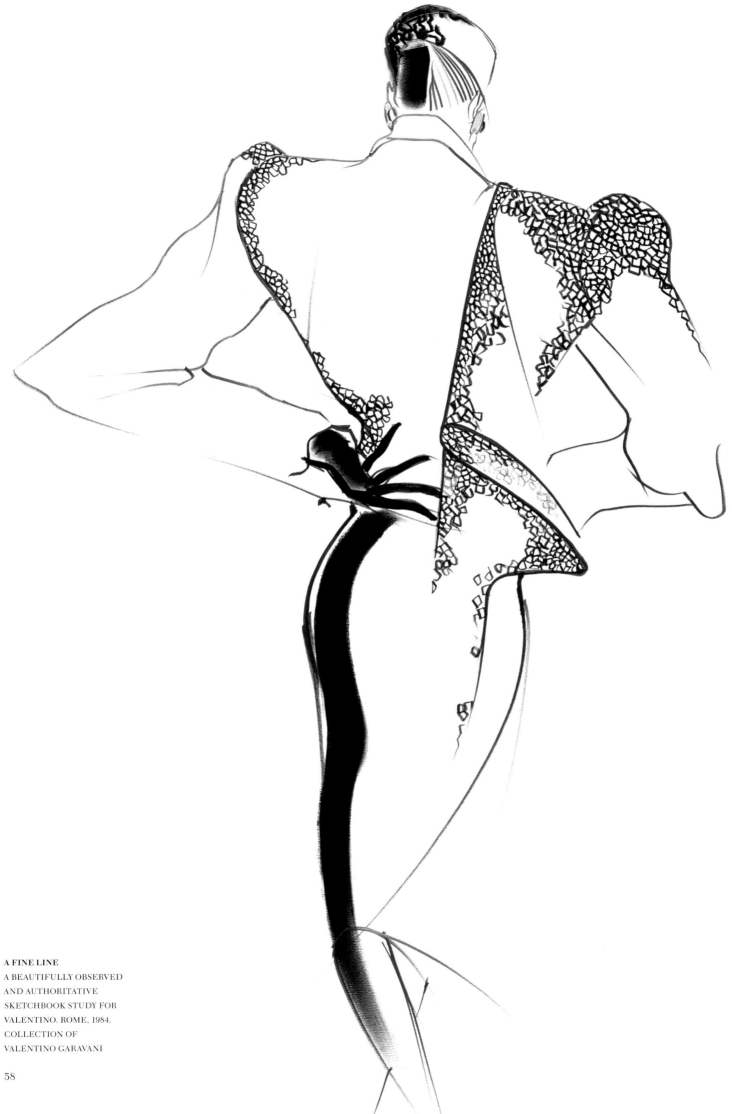

A FINE LINE
A BEAUTIFULLY OBSERVED
AND AUTHORITATIVE
SKETCHBOOK STUDY FOR
VALENTINO. ROME, 1984.
COLLECTION OF
VALENTINO GARAVANI

PICTURE PERFECT
TONY ALWAYS WORKED
WITH MODELS COIFFED
AND MADE-UP IN THE SAME
WAY AS IF THEY WERE
GOING ON SET FOR A
PHOTOGRAPHER. ROME, 1984.
COLLECTION OF VALENTINO
GARAVANI

STRETCHED
VIRAMONTES'S LONG,
ATTENUATED LINE
CELEBRATES VALENTINO'S
TASTEFUL BODY-CONSCIOUS
SILHOUETTE IN THIS
SKETCH, BEFORE IT
DISAPPEARS INTO THE
FOLDS OF A FULL AND
DRAMATICALLY CUT SKIRT.
ROME, 1984. COLLECTION
OF VALENTINO GARAVANI

OPPOSITE: **BLACK AND
WHITE**
DAY WEAR DETAILED IN
LIVELY CHALK LINES AND
DASHING FLOURISHES.
ROME, 1984. COURTESY OF
VOGUE ITALIA

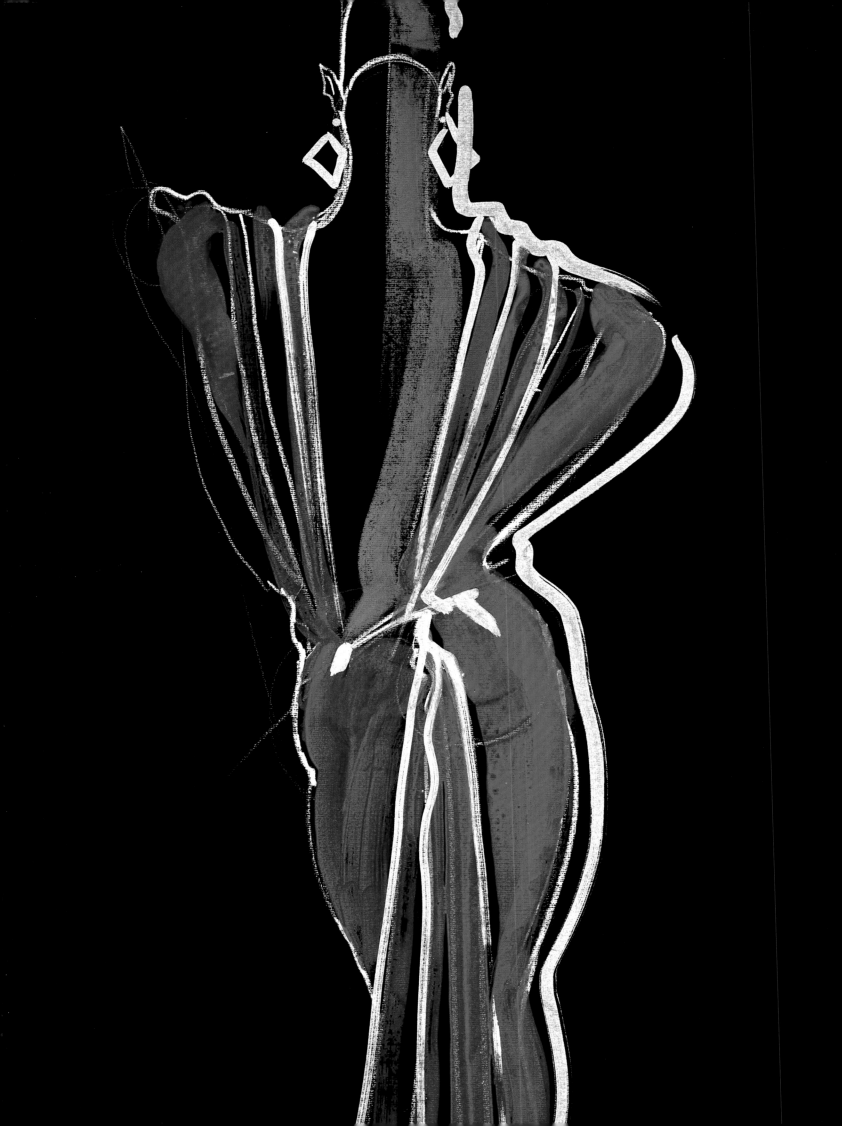

BEST FOOT FORWARD
ACCESSORIES SUCH AS
SHOES HAVE LONG BEEN
THE STOCK-IN-TRADE OF
THE FASHION ILLUSTRATOR.
VIRAMONTES ENLIVENS
WHAT COULD HAVE BEEN
A RATHER PEDESTRIAN
SKETCH WITH HIS SPIRITED
BRUSHWORK AND SIGNA-
TURE BRAVURA TECHNIQUE.
ROME, 1984. COLLECTION
OF VALENTINO GARAVANI

OPPOSITE: **LADY IN RED**
VALENTINO RED, HIS OWN
DISTINCTIVE AND SIGNA-
TURE HUE, FEATURED IN
EVENING WEAR AT EACH
OF HIS HAUTE COUTURE
PRESENTATIONS UNTIL
HIS RETIREMENT IN 2008.
ROME, 1984. COLLECTION
OF VALENTINO GARAVANI

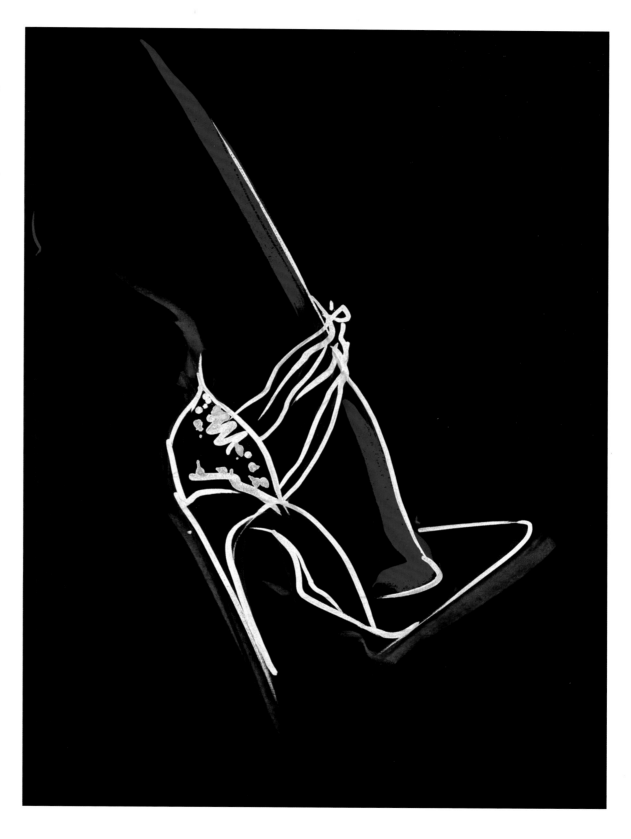

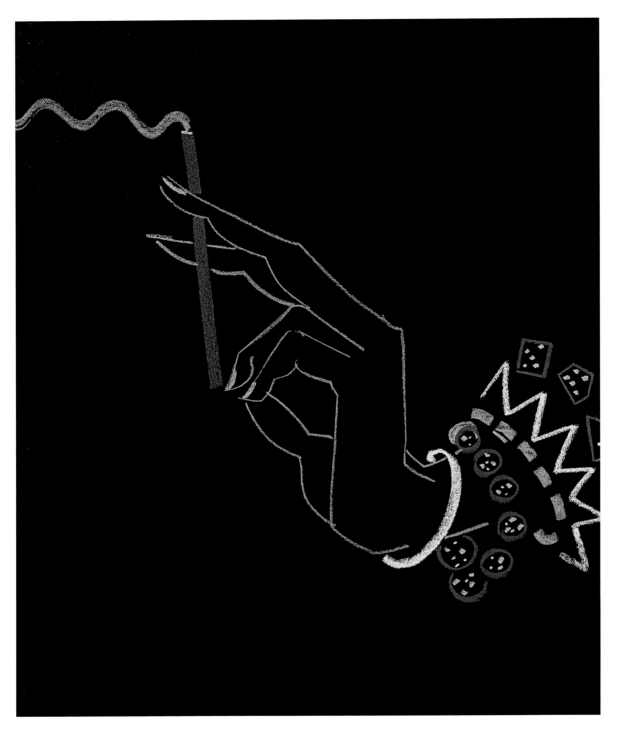

SOPHISTICATION AT HER FINGERTIPS
VIRAMONTES'S RICH, LUXURIOUS LINE EXTENDS ITSELF TO COSTUME JEWELLERY IN THIS JAUNTILY PATTERNED SKETCH. ROME, 1984. COLLECTION OF VALENTINO GARAVANI

OPPOSITE: **STARTING POINT** VIRAMONTES GIVES A NOD TO HIS MENTOR ANTONIO LOPEZ IN THIS SKETCH FOR VALENTINO. ROME, 1984

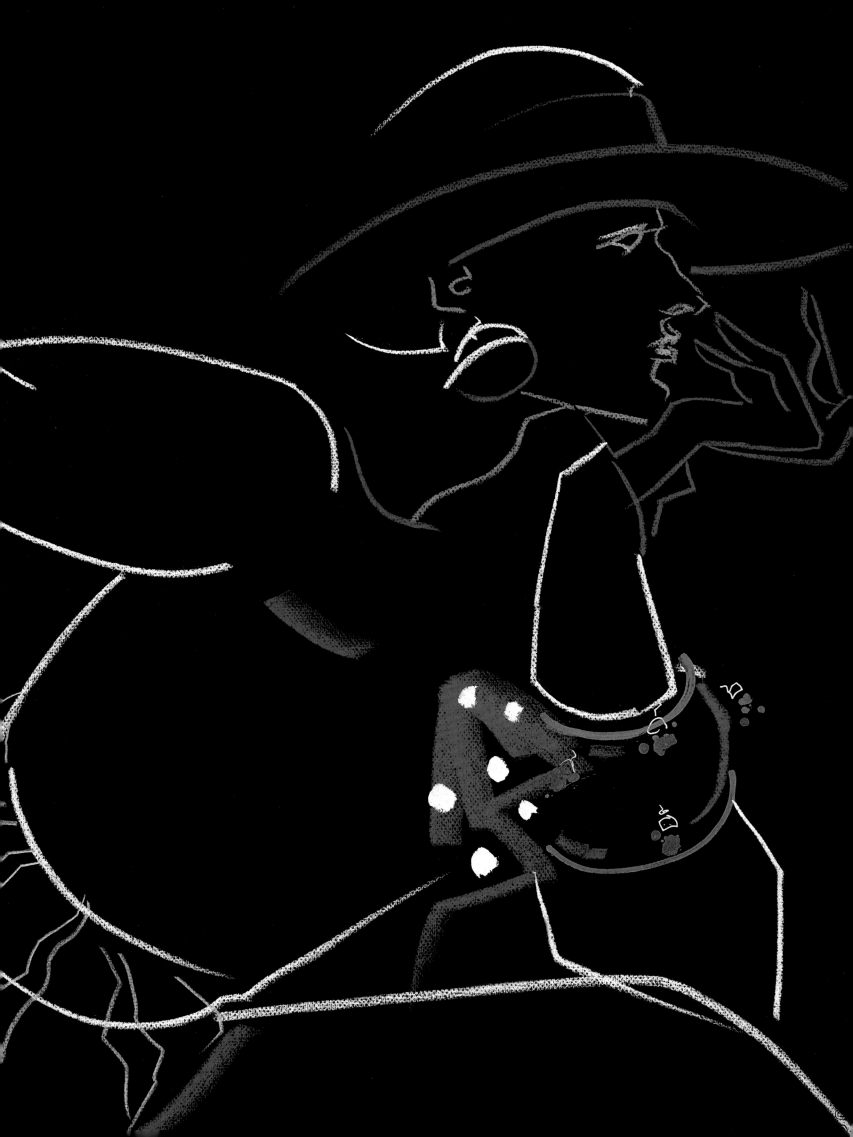

GLOWING COLOUR
A DAZZLING LUSHNESS AND
EFFORTLESS DRAUGHTS-
MANSHIP CHARACTERIZE
THESE TWO STUDIES FOR
VALENTINO. ROME, 1984.
COURTESY OF *VOGUE ITALIA*

SPOT THE DIFFERENCE
WITH WIT AND
ORIGINALITY, VIRAMONTES
CONJURES UP THE PLAYFUL
SPIRIT OF A POLKA DOT
DAY DRESS. ROME, 1984.
COURTESY OF *VOGUE ITALIA*

DRESS FOR SUCCESS
VIRAMONTES ALWAYS DREW
BIG, NEVER SMALL. IN THIS
SKETCH FOR VALENTINO
HE EXAGGERATES THE NEW
MASCULINE SILHOUETTE
THAT BEGAN TO EMERGE
IN THE 1980S. HASTILY, HE
DETAILS THE BROAD,
SQUARED-OFF SHOULDERS,
PINCHED-IN WAIST AND
SHORTER HEMLINES OF THE
MOMENT, EMPHASIZING THE
OUTLINE WITH A SINGLE
BORAD STROKE. ROME, 1984.
COLLECTION OF VALENTINO
GARAVANI

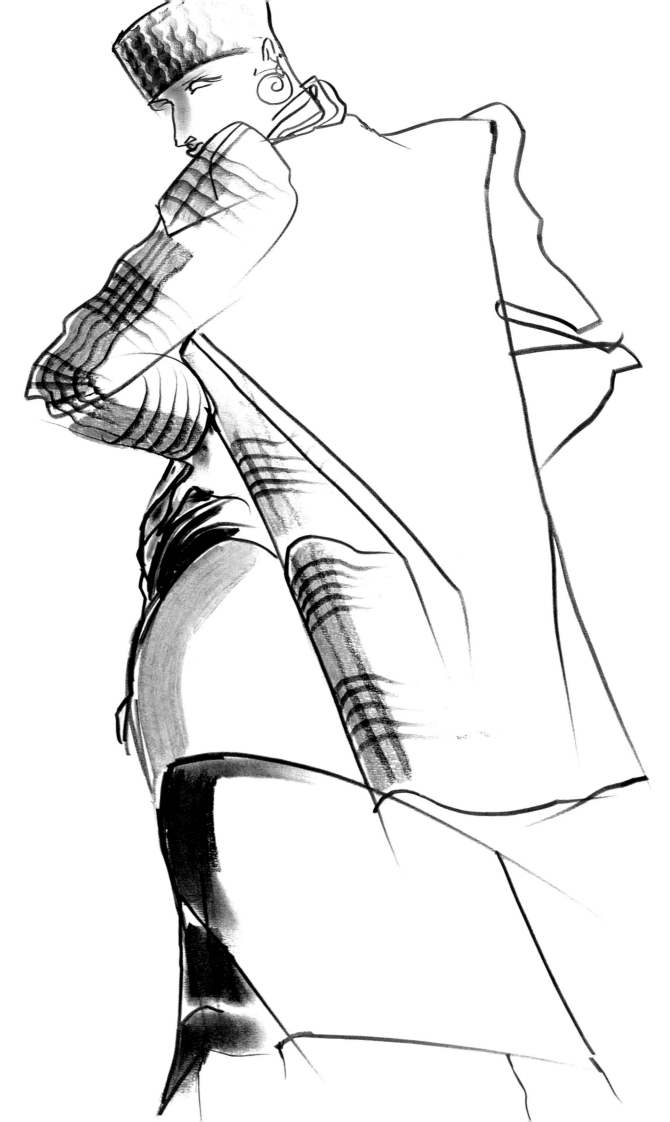

SKETCHBOOK
NOT CONCERNED WITH
DETAIL, VIRAMONTES CUTS
TO THE CHASE IN THIS
SKETCHBOOK STUDY FOR
VALENTINO, CAPTURING
THE ESSENCE OF THE
GARMENT IN AS FEW
STROKES AS POSSIBLE.
ROME, 1984. COLLECTION
OF VALENTINO GARAVANI

NO FRILLS
VIRAMONTES'S SHARP AND
INCISIVE LINE IS SIMPLE
AND DIRECT IN THIS
DYNAMIC SKETCH.
ROME, 1984. COLLECTION
OF VALENTINO GARAVANI

73

NIGHT AND DAY
A TYPICAL VALENTINO
PRESENTATION MIGHT
INCLUDE AS MANY AS 50
EVENING GOWNS WITH
ANOTHER 50 OR SO DAY
SUITS IN PASTEL WOOLS
AND CASHMERES. THE HARD
OUTLINES AND OVERT
GLAMOUR OF THE CLOTHES
LENT THEMSELVES
PERFECTLY TO TONY'S PEN
AND PAINTBRUSH. ROME,
1984. COLLECTION OF
VALENTINO GARAVANI

The name Pierre Cardin applies to a broad range of interests, but at the heart of the sprawling empire was once its eponymous creator's highly influential fashion designs. The minimal, graphic qualities of his clothes were underscored by a bold, frequently block-coloured or monochrome palette. Cardin was inventive and technically adept, a master cutter and constructor, creating garments that stood away from the body as seemingly independent sculptural objects.

PIERRE CARDIN

SLEEK CHIC
A FINE, FLUID
INTERPRETATION OF
PIERRE CARDIN'S SHARP
RIGOROUS RUFFLES FOR
MADAME FIGARO. PARIS, 1986

LOUIS FÉRAUD

Opening his first boutique in Cannes in 1950, Louis Féraud was recognized for the groomed elegance of his chic suits and sophisticated French tailoring. His slogan was 'Louis Feraud loves women'. Shot through with sex appeal, his clothes were worn regularly by Joan Collins during her *Dynasty* days and Brigitte Bardot started a craze for his girlish white sundresses. Féraud's head couture designer throughout the 1980s, Helga Björnsson, brought a touch of theatricality and inventiveness to the house.

FÉRAUD
ECONOMY OF LINE AND
VARIATIONS OF A SINGLE
TONE OF COLOUR CAPTURE
AN INTRINSICALLY ELEGANT
VIRAMONTES WOMAN
DRESSED IN FÉRAUD HAUTE
COUTURE. PARIS, 1984

DEXTER WONG

Malaysian-born Wong fed off club culture and the buzz of the streets when he arrived in London to study at Central Saint Martins in the early 1980s. His directional designs were produced in experimental fabrics with one eye to utility. Wong's first collection was picked up by London über PR Lynne Franks, and his clothes were soon gaining international attention, included with John Richmond, Betty Jackson and performance artist Leigh Bowery in a show organized by New York scene queen Suzanne Bartsch. Wong's look, stocked at HyperHyper, became synonymous with edgy but meticulous design, combining creativity and wearability.

DEXTER WONG FANCY BRUSHWORK CHARACTER-IZES THIS STUDY OF A DEXTER WONG ENSEMBLE FROM VIRAMONTES'S LONDON SKETCHBOOK FOR *HARPER'S BAZAAR*. LONDON, 1984

GIANNI VERSACE

The mistress to Armani's wife, as Anna
Wintour remarked, Gianni Versace was
unrivalled throughout the 1980s. There
was no other designer who announced
fashion to the world like Versace did –
perhaps because his style tended to be
loud, celebrating the theatrical and
beautiful. 'I want to be a designer for my
time,' he declared to *The New York Times*.
'I love the music, the art, the movies of
today. I want my clothes to express all of
this.' Executing his designs with unfailing
confidence, Versace's clothes were both
high fashion and haute couture, seamlessly
blending historical references with bold
geometric shapes.

IMPOSING STYLE
DRAWN FOR *VANITY*,
THE AVANT-GARDE AND
CULTISHLY COLLECTED
JOURNAL OF ANNA PIAGGI,
THIS UNUSUALLY
CONSERVATIVE ENSEMBLE
BY VERSACE IS LAID DOWN
WITH CONFIDENCE AND
STRONG BRUSHWORK.
MILAN, 1984

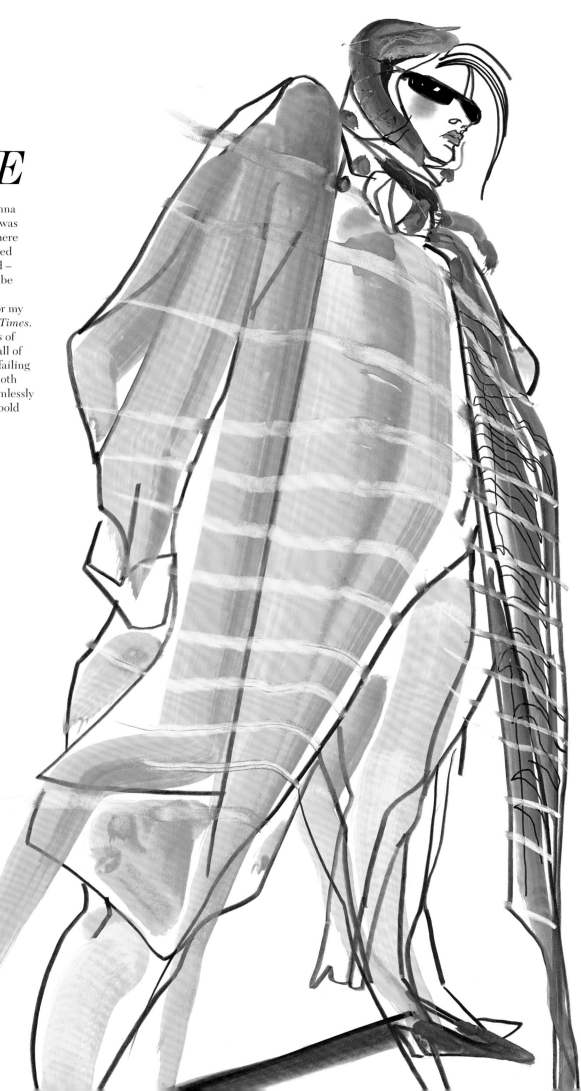

STRAIGHT TO THE POINT
VIRAMONTES KNEW HOW
TO CAPTURE THE MOOD
OF THE DESIGNERS HE
WORKED FOR. IN THIS
SKETCH FOR HANAE MORI,
A COUTURIER WHO
RESISTED FADS AND
TRENDS, HE RENDERS HER
SIGNATURE BUTTERFLY
MOTIF WITH A MINIMUM
OF FUSS IN SOFT PASTEL.
JAPAN, 1982. COLLECTION
OF HANAE MORI

OPPOSITE: **EXHIBITIONIST**
THE SEDUCTIVE MOVEMENT
OF TONY'S BRUSHWORK
COULD MAKE EVEN THE
SIMPLEST GARMENTS SING.
HERE HE WORKS HIS MAGIC
ON HANAE MORI'S PRÊT-À-
PORTER. JAPAN, 1984

BOTH IMAGES COURTESY
OF THE HANAE MORI
FOUNDATION.

HANAE MORI

Having established an atelier in 1951, Hanae Mori first
showed in New York in 1965 and opened her Maison
in Paris in 1977. Dubbed 'the Chanel of the East', she
was accepted into the Fédération Française de la
Couture, following highly successful showings in New
York and Paris. This ground-breaking accolade brought
an Asian woman into the heart of couture for the first
time and was tribute to Mori's abilities to merge the
finest traditions of design from two cultures – 'East
meets West' remains the concept behind the brand.
Forging her own path rather than following trends,
Mori combined classic European tailoring with the
colour palette and aesthetic ideals of her Japanese
inheritance, producing restrained, elegant and
beautifully cut designs.

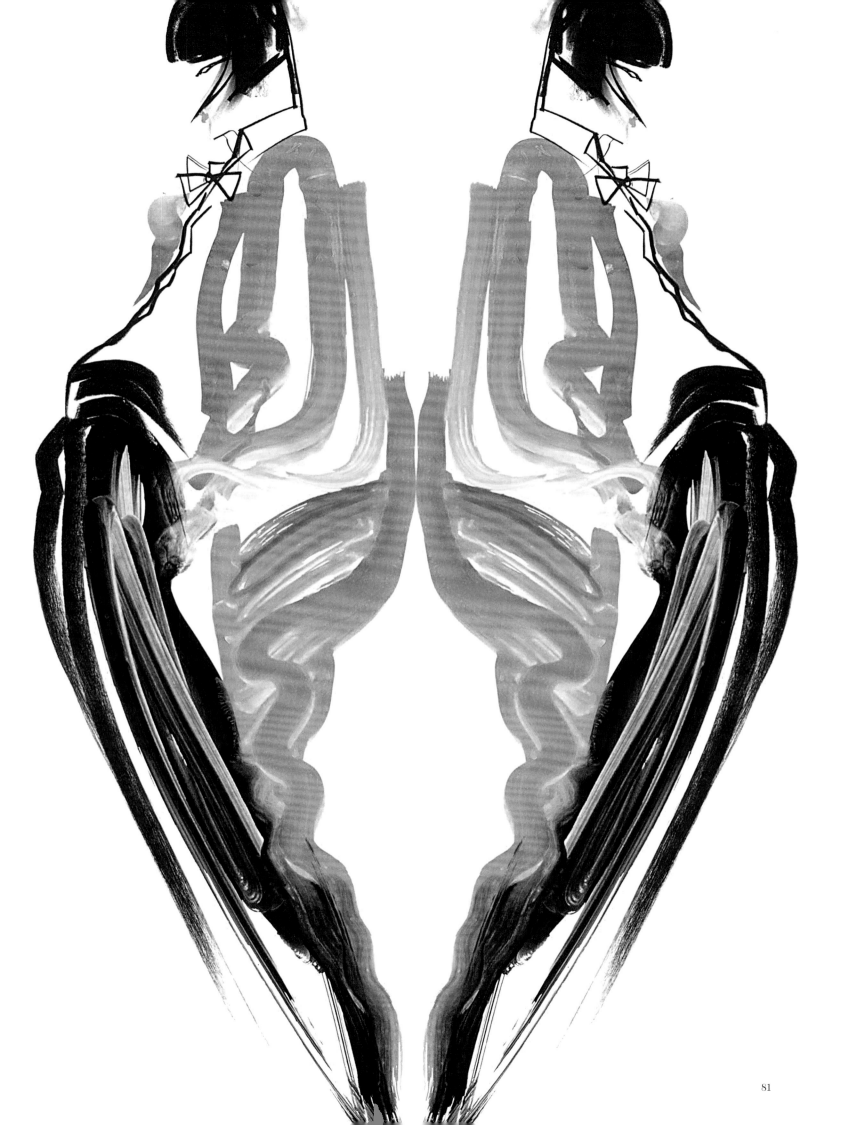

SIMPLE LUXE
STUDIED AND STYLIZED,
VIRAMONTES'S GRAPHIC
LINES WORK IN HARMONY
WITH ZORAN'S LUXURIOUS
MINIMALIST APPROACH TO
DESIGN. NEW YORK, 1980

ZORAN

A favourite designer of Viramontes, in line, look, colour,
theory and feeling, Zoran Ladicorbic has never been
a household name. The women who could afford his
luxurious Minimalism – Jackie Kennedy and Gloria
Vanderbilt amongst them – were. Placing function to the
fore, his clothes were cut and finished with obsession
and without any obvious fastenings. No buttons, zips or
other ties featured on his deceptively simple garments
constructed from luxurious silks and cashmere. His
debut monochrome collection from 1976 comprised
only five items. 'I am,' said Zoran, 'Gap for rich people.'

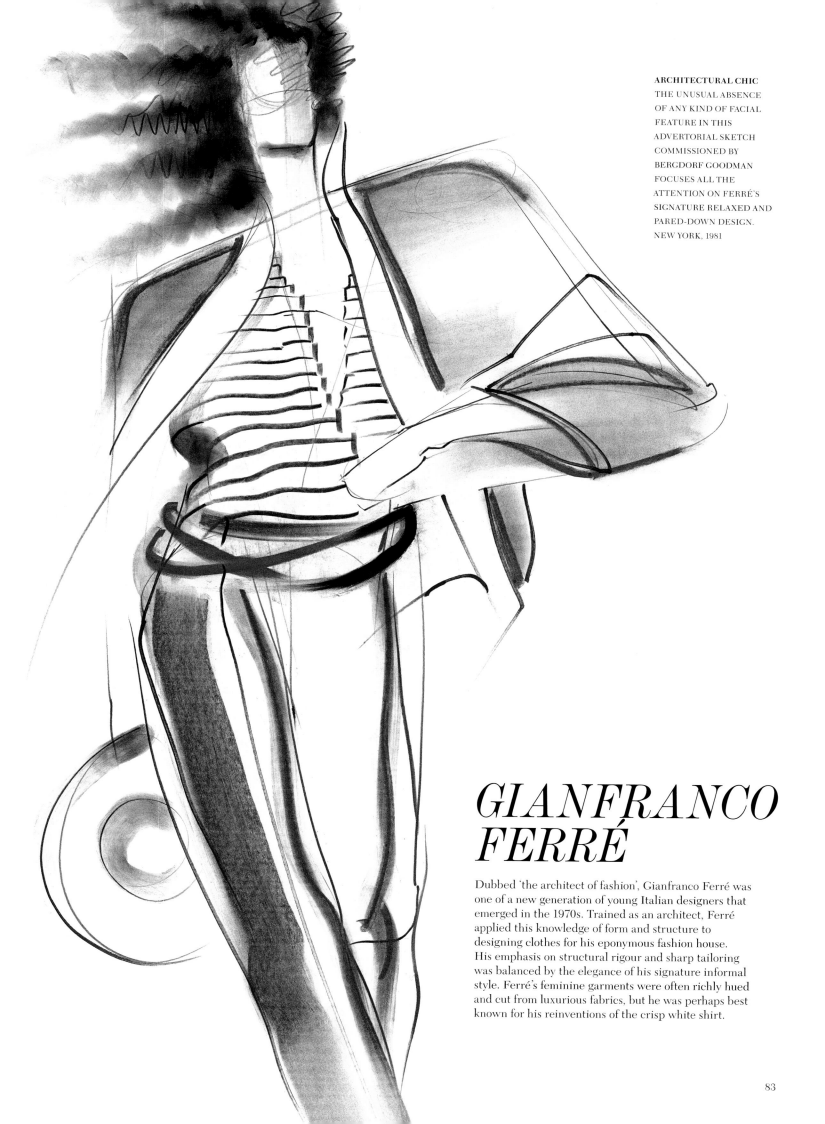

GIANFRANCO FERRÉ

Dubbed 'the architect of fashion', Gianfranco Ferré was one of a new generation of young Italian designers that emerged in the 1970s. Trained as an architect, Ferré applied this knowledge of form and structure to designing clothes for his eponymous fashion house. His emphasis on structural rigour and sharp tailoring was balanced by the elegance of his signature informal style. Ferré's feminine garments were often richly hued and cut from luxurious fabrics, but he was perhaps best known for his reinventions of the crisp white shirt.

HALSTON

Halston was the rock-star of American designers and the crown prince of New York nightlife. During the late 1960s and early 1970s he established a clean, fluid style of dressing that would become closely identified with the denizens of Studio 54. Working with cashmere, silk and Ultrasuede, Halston invented casual chic, that one-note look. To Halston less was more, producing simple cuts in a palette as selective as Mondrian's: he preferred a colour scheme of ivory, black and red. He once told *Vogue* that his role in fashion was to clean it up: 'just getting rid of all of the extra details that didn't work – bows that didn't tie, buttons that didn't button, zippers that didn't zip, wrap dresses that didn't wrap. I've always hated things that don't work.' His most successful clothes were imaginative variations on time-proven classics.

FLUID FASHION
THE LANGUID JET-SET GLAMOUR OF HALSTON'S DESIGNS HAS LONG SINCE BECOME PART OF THE FASHION LEXICON. HERE A BRIGADE OF HALSTONETTES MODEL KNITWEAR IN BLACK AND RED. PARIS, 1983

JEAN-LOUIS SCHERRER

A believer in evolution rather than revolution, Scherrer interpreted trends for the luxe market, embellishing or refining key looks to form his collections. His focus was on sumptuous fabrics and fine detailing and his affluent clients, who included Gettys, Rothschilds and Eastern royal families, appreciated his opulent approach, even to staples of daywear. His coats were trimmed with leather and fur; knitwear heavily appliquéd with velvets; his evening dresses were confections of chiffon and sequins; and, during the height of exuberant 1980s haute couture, he covered jackets and turbans with pearls and feathers.

PRINT PASSION
VIRAMONTES PROJECTS A GRAPHIC GLAMOUR IN THIS SKETCH OF JEAN-LOUIS SCHERRER HAUTE COUTURE. PICKING OUT BOLD PATTERN, THE INCREDIBLY DARK BRUSHSTROKES, ENGAGE THE NEGATIVE SPACE OF THE PAGE WITH FLAIR AND AUTHORITY. PARIS, 1984

SONIA RYKIEL

A proponent of uncomplicated comfort, known for her knitwear, Sonia Rykiel has become the very incarnation of French chic. Rykiel is Parisian chic, it is Left Bank chic. And to be even more precise, it is about Saint-Germain des Près. A forerunner of deconstruction and the minimalist style now championed by Rei Kawakubo and Martin Margiela, Rykiel has long been revelling in revealing the architecture of her garments – seams exposed, unlined – creating the *démodé* (undone) look. Add to that whimsical details such as lettering, rhinestones, lace, stripes and loads of black, and Rykiel style is born.

OPPOSITE:
DYNAMIC DÉMODÉ
THERE IS NOTHING STATIC IN VIRAMONTES'S ILLUSTRATIONS. IN THIS SKETCH FOR SONIA RYKIEL HIS ENERGY EXPLODES NOT ONLY IN HIS SENSE OF LINE, BUT ALSO IN THE IDEA OF MOVEMENT. PARIS, 1985

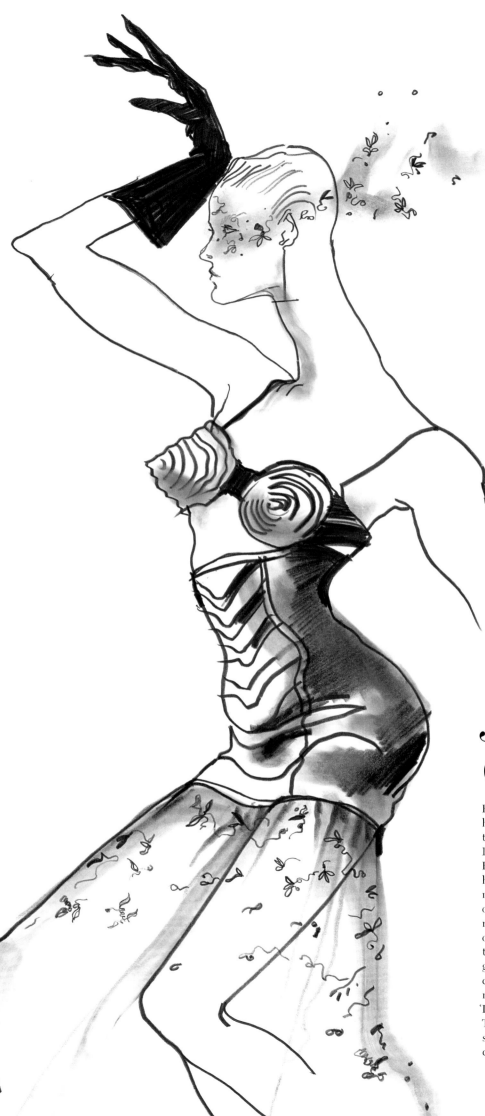

JEAN PAUL GAULTIER

Perhaps best known for the conical bras and basques
he conceived for Madonna's 1990 'Blonde Ambition'
tour, Jean Paul Gaultier emerged as a designer in the
1970s before launching his own fashion house in 1982.
His role as provocateur and *enfant terrible* of Parisian
haute couture stems from his irreverent attitude to its
more traditional looks. Early on he introduced a sense
of whimsy into his collections, a cheekiness that
remains as much a hallmark as his Breton tops (seen
on his perfume bottle Le Male) and reconstructed
trench coats. Always transgressive, he delights in
gender play, frequently dressing men in skirts and
corsetry while outfitting women in more conventionally
masculine attire. In *Interview* magazine he explained,
'I have never really cared about what fashion's ideal was.
There are different kinds of beauty and I always try to
show that.' Gaultier's clothes are always superbly
crafted and also fun.

STEPHEN JONES FOR JEAN
PAUL GAULTIER
THIS UNCOMPROMISINGLY
SHARP PROFILE BRINGS
TOGETHER A SLEEK,
ANGULAR LINE AND
MONOCHROMATIC PALETTE
THAT IS VERY VIRAMONTES.
MILLINER STEPHEN JONES
PROVIDED VIRAMONTES
WITH HATS THAT FIRED
HIS IMAGINATION AND
PROMPTED STYLIZED
INTERPRETATIONS.
PARIS, 1984

THIS PAGE AND OPPOSITE:
YSL RIVE GAUCHE
VIRAMONTES DID MORE
THAN JUST DRAW: HE
INTERPRETED, SIMPLIFYING
AND TRANSFORMING WHAT
HE SAW INTO A FIGURE THAT
CONVEYED IMMEDIATELY
HOW CLOTHES SHOULD BE
WORN. HERE HE DETAILS
YVES SAINT LAURENT'S
STYLISH OFF-THE-PEG SUITS,
WHICH BECAME A CENTRAL
THEME IN HIS COLLECTIONS
THROUGHOUT THE 1980S.
PARIS, 1983

YVES SAINT LAURENT

When Viramontes arrived in Paris one of his immediate goals was to sketch at the atelier of Yves Saint Laurent. Saint Laurent began his career as an assistant to Christian Dior in the 1950s and perhaps more than any other designer in Paris managed to survive the waning of couture culture without sacrificing his ideals or vision. Indeed, he spurred the rebirth of haute couture from its 1960 slump; from his Picasso-inspired dresses to his Pop Art and Ballets Russes collections, Saint Laurent drew from the past, reinterpreting it in a contemporary style. Always receptive to the changing demands of his clientele, he brought respectability to prêt-à-porter, establishing his Rive Gauche boutiques in 1966. Over his 45 years in fashion Saint Laurent changed the way women dressed, introducing safari suits and designing trousers for day or evening wear (most famously Le Smoking tuxedo suit). Yves Saint Laurent's innovative and rebellious colour combinations frequently brought out the best in Viramontes.

**YVES SAINT LAURENT
HAUTE COUTURE**
THE MODEL IS THE
DRAWING: VIRAMONTES
UNDERSTOOD THAT PEOPLE
GAVE LIFE TO THE CLOTHES
HE DREW. PARIS, 1984

ECONOMY OF LINE
DESIGNER STEPHEN
SPROUSE (THIS PAGE) AND
MUSE TERI TOYE (OPPOSITE)
POSED FREQUENTLY FOR
VIRAMONTES DURING
STEVEN MEISEL'S DRAWING
CLASSES AT PARSONS IN NEW
YORK. MEISEL ENCOURAGED
VIRAMONTES TO CAPTURE
THE ESSENCE OF A
GARMENT IN AS FEW MARKS
AS POSSIBLE. NEW YORK,
1983. COLLECTION OF
SYLVANA CASTRES

STEPHEN SPROUSE

An Indiana native, Stephen Sprouse cut his teeth at Halston before establishing his own label and creating clothes for Debbie Harry and Blondie. His first major collection in 1983 was a mash-up of the bold with the blasé, of punk's edginess with couture's classic lines. He favoured bright, Day-Glo, fluorescent colors, especially hot pink and yellow. He made mini dresses, mini skirts shown with bare midriffs, graffiti dresses and stockings.

PERRY ELLIS

Considered one of the original American designers, Perry Ellis created a distinctive look that helped to define America's place in the haute couture world. A new way of dressing, it broke from the traditions of Parisian fashion and its more stuffy overtones. His attitude to life and clothes was relaxed. Praised by critics and loved by consumers, Ellis's ability to innovate and invent produced clothes that were fresh and wearable versions of classic style. Ellis once said, 'My clothes are friendly – like people you've known for a long time, but who continue to surprise you.'

GENDER BENDING
DRAWN FOR *VOGUE ITALIA*,
LESLIE WINER MODELS
PERRY ELLIS MENSWEAR.
PARIS, 1984

OPPOSITE: **EARLY EDGE**
ONE OF VIRAMONTES'S
FIRST HIGH-PROFILE
CLIENTS WHEN HE
ARRIVED IN NEW YORK WAS
DESIGNER PERRY ELLIS.
NEW YORK, 1982

CLAUDE MONTANA

Claude Montana defined the power-dressing movement of the 1980s perhaps more than any other designer of the period. He was a leading advocate of the shoulder pad and its dramatic effects on proportion, which he often paired with oversized collars and striking colour. Montana pioneered body-conscious clothing that made women look bold and powerful. It was this exaggerated silhouette that brought him both criticism and acclaim. Leather was to become the signature, the code, the DNA of the Montana style: he manipulated it brilliantly, fashioning and embroidering it as if it were a soft, luxury fabric.

SUPER LUXE
THREE GRAPHITE STUDIES OF MONTANA DAYWEAR FROM VIRAMONTES'S SKETCHBOOK. PARIS, 1985

OVERLEAF: **RUNWAY**
IN PROVOCATIVE COUTURE AND STUNNINGLY PRODUCED SHOWS, CLAUDE MONTANA LED THE WAY. IN THIS INVITATION FOR THE DESIGNER'S ANNUAL RUNWAY PRESENTATION, VIRAMONTES INTRODUCES YVES KLEIN BLUE, A FAVORITE HUE OF THE COUTURIER. PARIS, 1985. COURTESY OF CLAUDE MONTANA

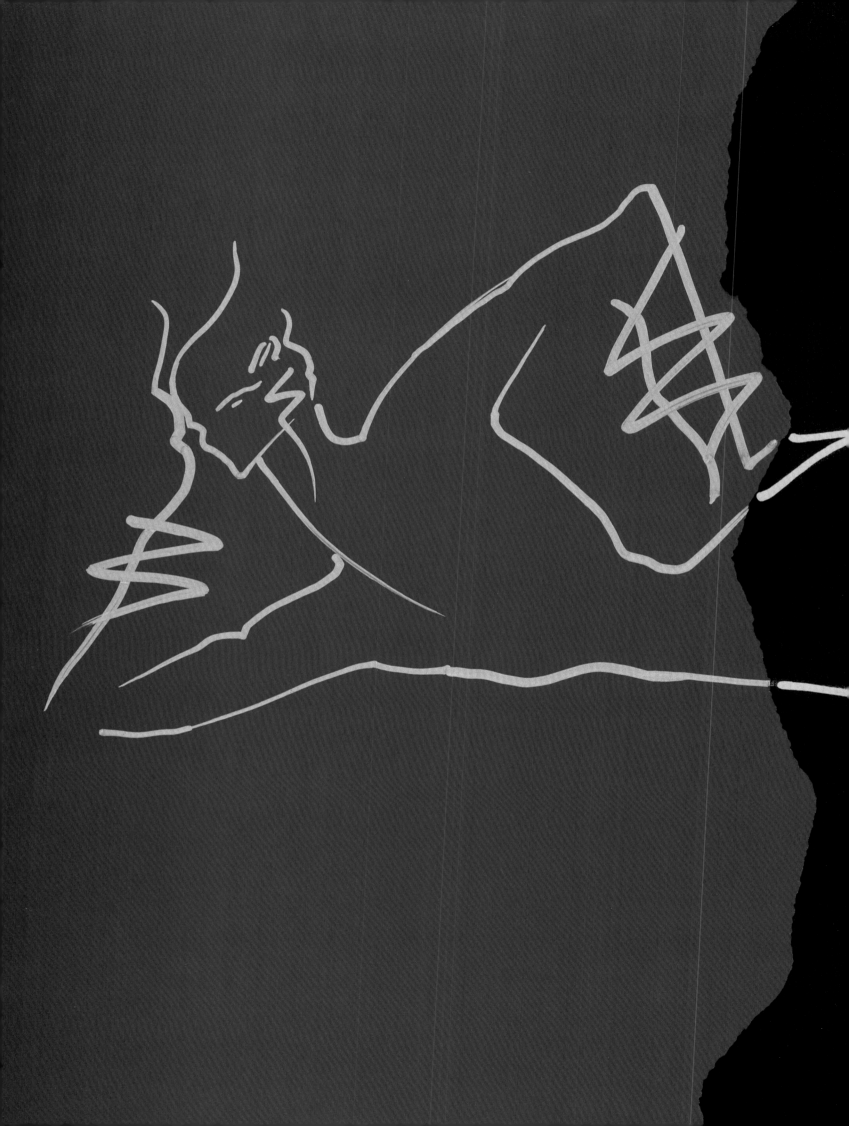

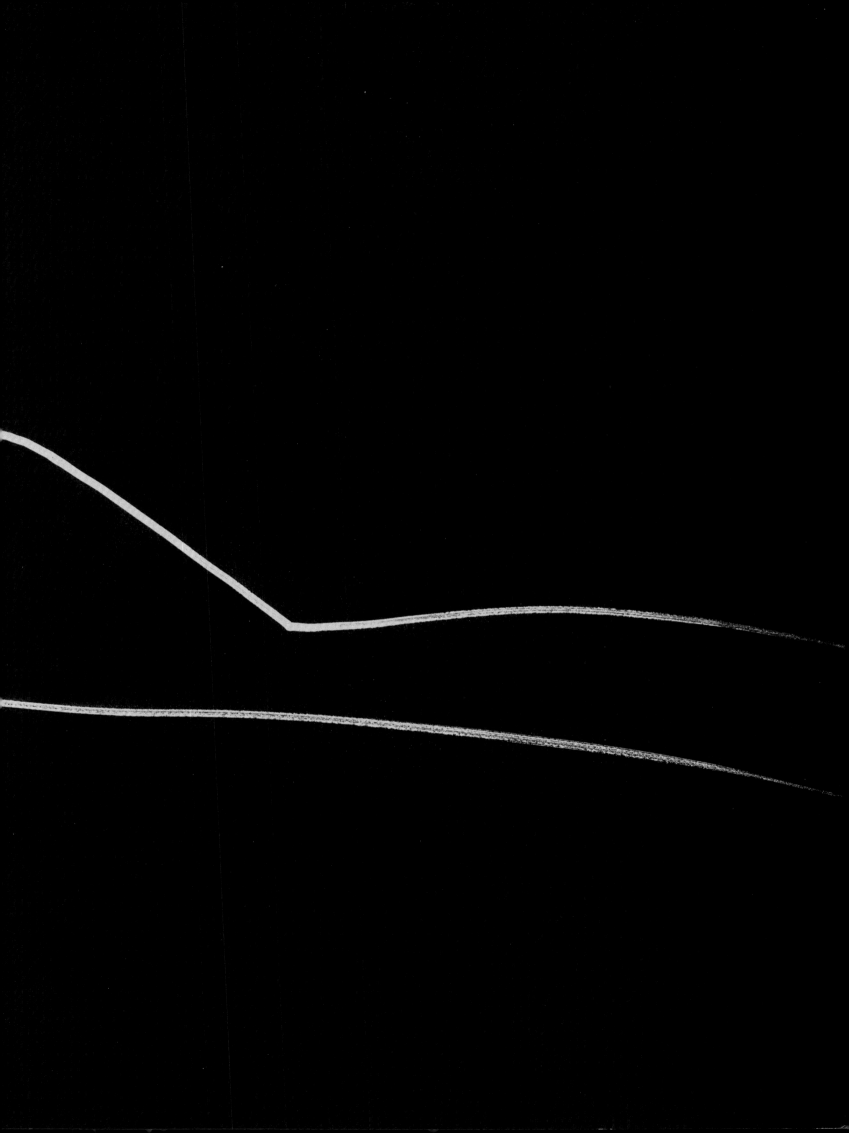

THEMES AND VARIATIONS
GLOVES BECAME PART OF
THE MONTANA SIGNATURE.
HERE VIRAMONTES
EXPLORES THE COUTURIER'S
TAKE ON A WARDROBE
STAPLE IN A SERIES OF
MONOCHROMATIC STUDIES.
JAPAN, 1984

JEAN BARTHET
A VIRAMONTES DRAWING
COULD BE AS WITTY AS IT
WAS STYLISH. HERE THE
ARTIST RECORDS THE
SENSE OF MISCHIEF
AND PLAYFULNESS IN
A FLOWERED HAT BY
JEAN BARTHET FOR
MONTANA. PARIS, 1984

104

PAULETTE
ACCESSORIES,
PARTICULARLY HATS,
ACHIEVED A NEW
IMPORTANCE IN THE
COLLECTIONS OF CLAUDE
MONTANA. IN THIS SKETCH
OF A HAT DESIGNED BY
PAULETTE MARCHAND,
VIRAMONTES'S LINE IS
CHARACTERISTICALLY
CONFIDENT. PARIS, 1984

STEPHEN JONES

Often called upon by designers who need hats to show their clothes to best advantage, since the early 1980s Stephen Jones has deftly reworked historical styles, in the process making them utterly contemporary. His idiosyncratic hats range from dramatic couture conversation pieces to accessible, chic headwear. In June 1982 *Vogue*'s Liz Tilberis referred to Jones as 'a new breed of milliner, whose talent incorporates anything from show-hat splendour to pull-on simplicity'. His often asymmetric and quirky hats quickly became popular with designers such as Claude Montana and Thierry Mugler. In 1984, Jones became the first British milliner to work in Paris, where he created the hats for Jean Paul Gaultier's catwalk presentation.

SIBYLLE DE SAINT PHALLE
SWISHY BRUSHSTROKES AND GENTLE GRAPHITE DETAILING LEND A SPONTANEOUS AIR TO THIS PORTRAIT OF THE ARISTOCRATIC SIBYLLE DE SAINT PHALLE. AN EARLY MUSE TO MILLINER STEPHEN JONES, VIRAMONTES DECLARED THAT 'SIBYLLE WAS BORN TO WEAR A HAT'. JONES DESCRIBED THE PARISIAN FASHIONISTA AS 'IMPOSSIBLY GLAMOROUS'. LONDON, 1984. COURTESY OF SIBYLLE DE SAINT PHALLE

CLAUDIA HUIDOBRO
A THOUGHTFUL AND DIRECT
CHARCOAL STUDY OF
CLAUDIA HUIDOBRO IN A
HAT DESIGNED BY STEPHEN
JONES. PARIS, 1984

ISSEY MIYAKE

Issey Miyake is a designer known for his innovative, experimental fabrics and use of cutting-edge technology. Graduating from Tokyo's Tama Art University in 1964 he then spent several years working in the fashion hubs of New York and Paris (with Guy Laroche, Hubert de Givenchy and Geoffrey Beene), before returning to his native Japan and presenting his first collection under the label Issey Miyake in 1971. His conceptual pieces often transformed cloth into corrugated, quilted and curled shapes, which he later developed into a method of permanently pleating fabric. Always striving to reconcile form and function, while his work is grounded in his craftsmanship it thrives on his continual quest for the perfect proportion and forces people to look at clothing in a new way.

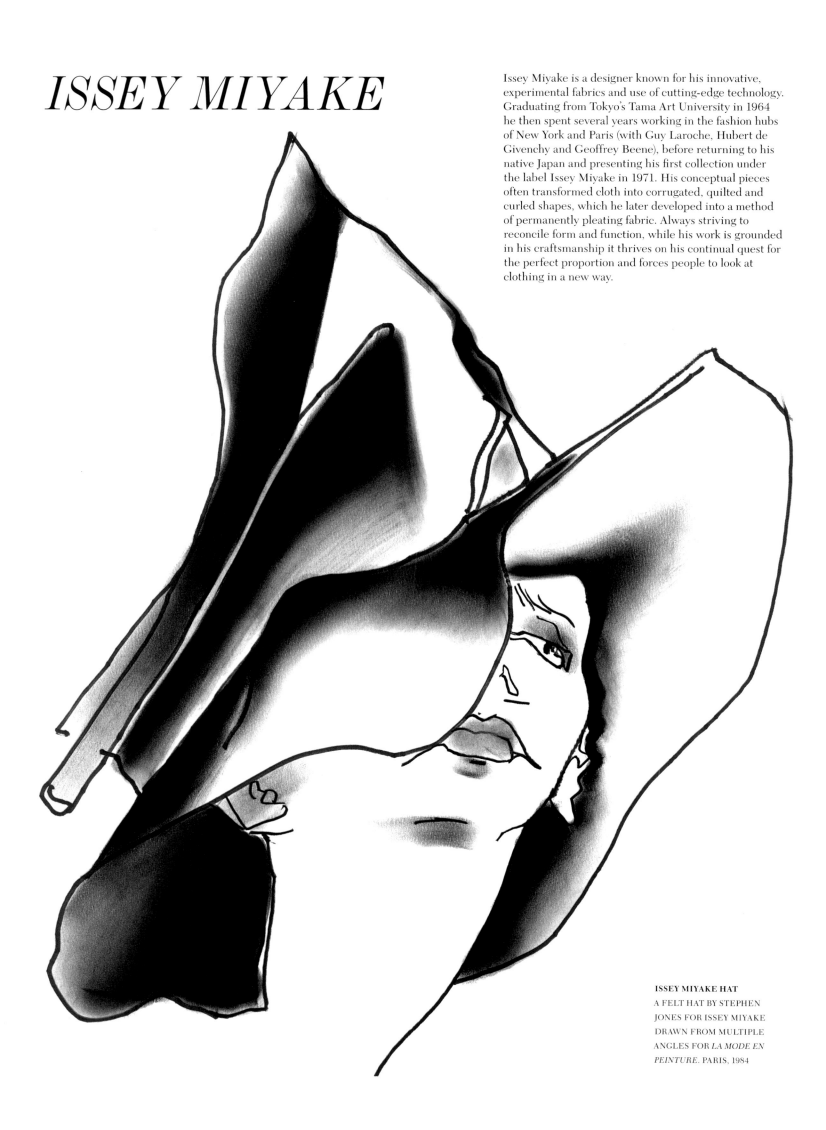

ISSEY MIYAKE HAT
A FELT HAT BY STEPHEN JONES FOR ISSEY MIYAKE DRAWN FROM MULTIPLE ANGLES FOR *LA MODE EN PEINTURE*. PARIS, 1984

ON WOMEN

'I need a model to see and create. I can't just imagine.'

VIRAMONTES

Casting was very important to Viramontes. When Tony looked for a model he was not just looking for a standard set of measurements or a conventionally beautiful face; these were not enough. He liked to be inspired by his girls. Only women who really impressed him had any chance of finding themselves featured in his work. Viramontes had begun to create his own pantheon of heroines as a teenager. Those whose allure and charisma spoke directly to his imagination stood out, those willing to lend their style, bodies and faces to him: unusual demands in an age when models were meant to be little more than hangers for the garments they wore.

It is no accident that each of Viramontes's girls was blessed with a face that made for dramatic line drawings; he threw open the door for a new breed of woman to appear in the fashion pages. His choice of models redefined beauty to encompass girls with exotic or different looks. In fact he invented a certain kind of woman: like all models she had incredibly long legs and stood over eight heads high, but her pose and attitude monopolized the imagination of the period. Viramontes crystallized an image of femininity that was to become emblematic of the 1980s. Rather than simply flaunting her femininity, there was a certain insolence about the Viramontes woman.

Each of Tony's girls adopted an air that was confident and aloof, nonchalant, even a little haughty. You need only see a face once to know it was a Viramontes face, a Viramontes model. They were not pretty faces: they were strong, with a full mouth, a prominent nose and graphic brow. There was a diabolical grace in what Viramontes drew. He focused, subtly and delicately, on what made a woman different or unusual. 'What Tony did so beautifully was to cultivate and train his models,' remembers hairdresser Bob Recine. 'He favoured those willing to let themselves be shaped and moulded into whatever he was looking for. They had to be willing to bleach their hair, to shave their eyebrows, to be a blank canvas dedicated to whatever he was trying to create.' Unlike many fashion illustrators who sketched from photographs, Tony always worked from life.

However stylized his finished drawings might be, they were always based on a real girl. Violeta Sanchez, perhaps his most frequent leading lady, suggests it was more interesting and amusing to him to draw from life. 'You always imagine that someone who draws can do so from their imagination (and they can) but it's much more fun to draw from a fully finished model. It can take you in directions that you might not have thought of going yourself.' Similarly, Bob Recine recalls that Tony very rarely drew without hair and make-up: 'I never remember him doing any drawings without a team helping him to prepare the look.' Tony wanted the look in front of him as close as possible to how he imagined the drawings. 'He didn't dream with his pencil, he dreamed in the reality of what he was creating first. He didn't want to alter what he saw; he would accentuate or exaggerate, but he was very particular about finishing this creature as a true entity before he would begin.'

One of his greatest strengths lay in his relationship with his sitters. Model Janice Dickinson remembers how Viramontes pulled together her look, dressing her like a supermodel dandy. 'It was a partnership,' she recalls, 'we enabled one another. Tony painted my face, styled my hair, he put me in lady, lady heels with little ankle socklettes. He got me ready and we danced out together.'

If Tony's drawings often seemed more about the person wearing the clothes than the actual garments, it is because he believed that it is the individual who puts a signature on a garment and not a designer. Tony was inspired by people; people were what he loved more than anything else. 'He drew people,' says Dickinson,

'not models as coat hangers.' Viramontes understood that people brought life to the clothes he drew, that style is not just how you wear clothes – it is about the way you walk, talk, dance and prance. Add to that the right face and the picture is completed. Tony's most successful drawings were not bland amalgams or expressionless blanks but always invested with real personalities.

The lifestyle and type of woman he envisioned in his sketches gives his work a spark of amazing energy. His models were often people he knew well, such as Teri Toye, Leslie Winer and Violeta Sanchez. This level of intimacy is apparent and is a contributing factor to the success of his work. The way he saw these women wear clothes reveals far more than the fabric alone was capable of revealing, his dressed figures communicating immediately how clothes should be worn.

Viramontes fixed on paper an attitude – the tilting of the head, the movement of the hip – his detailed delineations all but tell us what the sitter is thinking. But working with Tony was tough. 'It was very intense,' remembers model agent Cyril Brulé. 'He would work for hours, making a girl hold a pose, they had to have stamina. But he would involve them in the work; they felt like it was teamwork. I think that people liked that. A lot of the time when you pose and model you do not have much involvement in the creativity of the process. Today even less than before, everyone is looking at the computer and no one is looking at the model.' With Tony there was a complicity, an extraordinary collaboration. He and the model would work together on gestures and body language. It was almost like choreography. But it was never a smooth or tranquil path, says Recine. 'Tony usually was not happy until someone was crying or complaining, or something would explode emotionally. I think that was his affirmation that he had created something that was authentic.'

PREVIOUS SPREAD AND OPPOSITE:
A WORK OF ART
A DARK, ZAFTIG BEAUTY WITH BLUE-BLACK HAIR, PALOMA HAD A PROFILE MADE FOR CHARCOAL AND A REPUTATION THAT PRECEDED HER. TONY SPENT A MEMORABLE AFTERNOON AT THE HISTORIC HÔTEL GEORGE V IN PARIS SKETCHING PICASSO'S DAUGHTER FOR A FEATURE IN BRITISH *VOGUE* WHILE DAVID BAILEY PHOTOGRAPHED HER. PARIS, 1983. VOGUE © THE CONDÉ NAST PUBLICATIONS LTD

PALOMA PICASSO

The daughter of artist Pablo Picasso, Paloma loomed over the international worlds of fashion, art and society throughout the 1980s. Visually arresting, her aggravated, scornful-looking lips and angular profile served as a reminder of her father's Cubist inclinations. Picasso stood out amongst her peers, exuding a heady mixture of both grace and menace, femininity and masculinity – and sexuality. Viramontes adored her. For years a stimulating client of some of the world's greatest couturiers, Picasso, who habitually clothed herself in red, black and gold, eventually became a designer herself. Tony drew her many times, first in New York and then in Paris at the height of her popularity as a jewellery designer for Tiffany & Company.

SCARLETT NAPOLEON BORDELLO

Poster girl for fashion's underground fast set, Scarlett Napoleon Bordello was a hostess and door whore at Cha Cha's, a gay disco in the back room at London nightclub Heaven; she hung out with Leigh Bowery and Trojan. A thin willowy girl with a face verging on the plain, she styled herself in such an incredible way that she always looked compelling. With lips painted in a taut cupid's bow and an asymmetric shark-fin quiff, she described herself as 'a model-come-artist's accessory'. Fashion editor Hamish Bowles recalls her habit of holding a hand mirror up to those who failed to meet her uncompromising sartorial standards, uttering the devastating line, 'Would you let yourself in?' Viramontes found her irresistible and drew her frequently.

SCARLETT NAPOLEON BORDELLO

NO MATTER HOW EDGY OR STREET THE MODEL, VIRAMONTES'S SUBJECTS WERE ALWAYS BEAUTIFULLY OBSERVED. HERE HIS ELEGANT AND REDUCTIVE BRUSH EFFORTLESSLY CAPTURES CLUB-KID SCARLETT'S STRIKING LOOK. LONDON, 1984

NAOMI CAMPBELL

British supermodel Naomi Campbell's exotic mix of Jamaican and Chinese ancestry propelled her onto magazine covers the world over. Prowling and self-confident, a young Naomi Campbell was introduced to Viramontes by Cyril Brulé. At the beginning of her own career and on her first trip to Paris the 16-year-old Campbell spent an afternoon posing at Viramontes's chic Avenue de Saxe apartment in a tutu by Azzedine Alaïa. Naomi was young enough not to get tired or complain, remembers Bob Recine, and just to be excited to have someone draw her.

THIS SPREAD AND
OVERLEAF:
FASHION FORWARD
BROAD, EVEN
BRUSHSTROKES WERE
THE STARTING POINT FOR
THIS SLINKY SILHOUETTE
OF NAOMI CAMPBELL.
VIRAMONTES'S SIMPLE
OUTLINES LEND A CASUAL,
SPONTANEOUS AIR
TO THESE DRAWINGS
OF THE 1980s BLACK
SUPERMODEL. PARIS, 1985

LISA ROSEN

'It' girl Lisa Rosen was an achingly hip fixture on the downtown New York scene that fused the worlds of art and music. Hanging out at the Mudd Club, Rosen was both a participant and a muse. Her career as a model began by chance when stylist Patricia Field lent her a one-way ticket to Paris and a Chanel scout sent her down the runway. After Chanel 'I got everybody. I did shows for Dior, Mugler, Jean Paul Gaultier, Yamamoto, blah, blah, blah.' She was the embodiment of the New Wave style and nonchalant attitude of the moment. Rosen's look – pallid face framed by raven hair, expressive mouth – drove Viramontes crazy.

ABOVE: POLAROID BY VIRAMONTES. NEW YORK, c. 1985

OPPOSITE:
MODEL ATTITUDE
'TONY LIKED VERY EXAGGERATED EXPRESSIONS,' REMEMBERS LISA ROSEN, 'SUPER-WIDE SMILES OR YOUR MOUTH YELLING "ARHHHHHHH!"'
HERE SHE POSES FOR A PAUL GOBAL MAKE-UP STUDY. PARIS, 1985

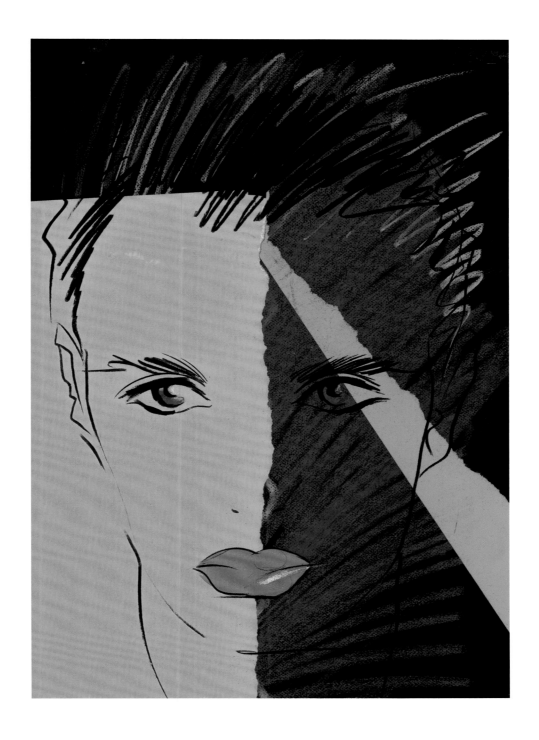

ISABELLA ROSSELLINI

Dubbed one of the most beautiful people in the world by *People* magazine, ravishing Rossellini, the daughter of Italian film director Roberto Rossellini and Swedish screen siren Ingrid Bergman, began her modelling career at the comparatively late age of 28. Her sleek and simple appearance was a marked contrast to many girls of the day and she quickly became one of the foremost faces of the 1980s, racking up no fewer than 28 international *Vogue* covers, including nine shot by Richard Avedon. Her big break came in 1982 when she began a 14-year tenure as the face of Lancôme. In 1986 Rossellini's starring role in David Lynch's film *Blue Velvet* was the genesis of an avant-garde screen career.

ROSSELLINI COLLAGE

VIRAMONTES EMPLOYS A HEADY MIXTURE OF COLLAGE AND DRAWING TO GREAT EFFECT IN THIS PORTRAIT OF ISABELLA ROSSELLINI. PARIS, 1985

OPPOSITE:

ESSENTIAL BEAUTY

A CHARCOAL SKETCHBOOK STUDY OF ISABELLA ROSSELLINI. PARIS, 1985

'He did my hair like no one else could; he would use Brylcreem and coconut oil to achieve that perfect Viramontes shine.'

JANICE DICKINSON

JANICE DICKINSON

The world's first self-proclaimed supermodel, Janice Dickinson redefined American beauty at a time when the fashion pages were populated by classic blue-eyed blondes. Leaving Florida for New York after winning national competition Miss High Fashion in the early 1970s, Dickinson discovered that her looks – sensuous bee-stung lips and large brown eyes – did not fit the current mould. Undeterred, she left for Paris where she scored an immediate success and built up a portfolio as thick as a phone book. By the time she met Viramontes in the 1980s Dickinson was a well-known face and name, and had appeared on the cover of *Vogue* some 37 times.

ABOVE: POLAROIDS BY VIRAMONTES. NEW YORK, c. 1982

OPPOSISTE:
SUPERMODEL SNARL
A SERIES OF SWIFT, RIGOROUS BRUSHSTROKES ARE LAID DOWN WITH CONFIDENCE IN THIS PORTRAIT OF MODEL JANICE DICKINSON. NEW YORK, 1982

LESLIE WINER

Leslie was the top model of the early 1980s, remembers British milliner Stephen Jones. 'She alternately inspired and terrified the fashion world.' A heroin-chic model before the term was known and a great provocatrice, she developed a reputation for being difficult to work with. Tony drew her many times, first in Paris for British *Vogue*, then in London and Japan at the height of her popularity as a model. 'I love her movement, her attitude,' he confided to his diary. Viramontes was attracted to her strong, androgynous features and willingness to hold still for as long as it took to get it right. Having posed for both Jean-Michel Basquiat and Salvador Dalí, Leslie was a true artist's model, not too tall, not too thin and with an air of unmistakable hauteur. Leslie was a Viramontes drawing come to life, the epitome of the Viramontes woman.

ABOVE: POLAROIDS BY VIRAMONTES. PARIS, c. 1983

OPPOSITE:
A HEAD FOR HATS
TOUGH AND OTHER-WORLDLY, BUT ALWAYS IN VOGUE (AND IN *VOGUE*), LESLIE WINER SPORTS A COCKTAIL HAT BY MILLINER STEPHEN JONES. 'THE HAT PERFECTLY REFLECTED HER CHARAC-TER,' SAID JONES OF THE TIP-TILTED TRILBY IN LEATHER AND CHANTILLY LACE. PARIS, 1983.
VOGUE © THE CONDÉ NAST PUBLICATIONS LTD

'*I looked like a boy in normal life. So modelling was kinda like dressing up. I think Tony took a little bit of pleasure in the idea that someone who looked like a boy could put on a dress, these ridiculous hats and make-up. It was like drag.*'

LESLIE WINER

ANGULAR ANDROGYNY
VIRAMONTES'S RAZOR-LIKE LINES CAPTURE A NONCHALANT AND OFF-DUTY LESLIE WINER IN THIS SKETCHBOOK STUDY. PARIS, 1985

OPPOSITE: **BEAUTY CONTEST** WITH THEIR FIERY RED LIPS AND LACQUERED FINGERNAILS, TONY'S GIRLS OFTEN HAD FACIAL EXPRESSIONS MORE COMMONLY FOUND IN THE PAGES OF PORNOGRAPHIC MAGAZINES THAN THE FASHION PAGES OF *VOGUE*. HERE, LESLIE WINER'S SLIGHTLY PARTED LIPS AND SMOKY EYES PREVIEW HELENA RUBENSTEIN'S LATEST COLOUR PALETTE FOR *LA MODE EN PEINTURE*. PARIS, 1984

TERI TOYE

*'I think it was
more about my look.
Which was kind of
1960s, edgy, that whole
Stephen Sprouse
New York street look
that he liked.'*

TERI TOYE

Tall, blonde and stunning, Teri Toye arrived in New York from Des Moines, Iowa, as a boy and slowly began to transition into a girl. After a brief stint at Parsons she quit class to become the poster girl for downtown cool, slowly but surely emerging as a fully-fledged fashion megastar and 'it' girl. A favourite model and muse of designer Stephen Sprouse, Toye's reputation was sealed in 1984 when *The New York Times* fashion columnist John Duka named her Girl of the Year. She didn't look back. 'There were people who were mortified by Teri,' remembers hairdresser Bob Recine, 'and would refuse to work with her. Then there were people like Tony, Karl Lagerfeld and Jean Paul Gaultier who were enthralled by her.' Teri came to Paris, to the delight of Tony. Here was someone extremely special, beautiful, dangerous and taboo: all the elements that Tony admired and strove to convey in his work.

ABOVE LEFT: POLAROID BY VIRAMONTES. NEW YORK, c. 1982

ABOVE RIGHT AND OPPOSITE:
ALL ABOUT TERI
VIRAMONTES GRAPHICALLY DESCRIBES TOYE'S SIGNATURE DEADPAN GLAMOUR IN THESE CHARCOAL STUDIES. NEW YORK, 1983

OVERLEAF:
BODY CONSCIOUS
ATTITUDE AND LOOK COME FIRST IN THESE STUDIES OF TERI TOYE. THE CLOTHES BY STEPHEN SPROUSE ALMOST SEEM TO BE A SECONDARY CONSID- ERATION. NEW YORK, 1983

'I always hated my photographs. At that time I really just hated to look in the mirror! One of the only things I liked were Tony's renditions of me and his idea of the way he felt that I looked. I always thought, "Wow, I wish I looked liked that!" I was always so flattered.'

RENÉ RUSSO

RENÉ RUSSO

Spotted at a Rolling Stones concert in 1972, René Russo was snapped up by the Ford Modelling Agency, and within the year appeared on the cover of *Vogue* and became the face of Revlon Cosmetics. As far as Tony was concerned, Russo was in a class of her own. 'He was obsessed with René,' remembers childhood friend Julie Rosenbaum, 'he drew her all the time and would haunt the newsstand on Las Palmas hoping to find pictures of her in the latest *Vogue*.' Then he saw her one day in Westwood, so he went up to her and to her and introduced himself. '"I think you're beautiful and I would love to paint you," he told her. They got together and they became friends.' Russo remembers Viramontes as a kindred spirit. 'He was born and raised in Los Angeles,' she recalls, 'we were both outsiders, kind of mutts, neither of us come from money. He was so ballsy and aggressive but sweet. He just came right up to me in Westwood and won me over. I clicked with him.' He did a lot of pencil work at this time, adds Rosenbaum, that was much softer than his later work; it did not have the hard edges for which he was to become so well known. 'René had such severe bone structure that he would draw her softly and beautifully. He was into anything severe with hard edge and she had the cheekbones. He hated the cute blonde girls that were popular then.'

ABOVE: POLAROIDS BY VIRAMONTES. NEW YORK, c. 1981

OPPOSITE: **AN IDEAL WOMAN** IN HIS EARLIEST PAINTINGS VIRAMONTES ACTED AS HIS OWN STYLIST, IMPROVISING EACH LOOK. HERE HE PAINTED MODEL RENÉ RUSSO IN A MAURY HOPSON HEADSCARF WITH AN ALMOST DOCUMENTARY-LIKE REALISM, CAREFULLY RECORDING EACH DETAIL. LOS ANGELES, 1979

'Tony's drawings of me always have an element of mystery. Working with an artist is very different from working with a photographer. A photograph is bound by being a single moment captured in a frame where an artist has more freedom to work with time and depth.'

KAREN BJORNSON

KAREN BJORNSON

Bjornson was having little success as a model until the day her agent Wilhelmina sent her to see the designer Roy Halston. Rail-thin, with narrow shoulders, long legs and bright blue eyes, Bjornson was to become the designer's in-house model and constant companion. Halston transformed the former Miss Cincinnati from an all-American beauty queen into the personification of Upper East Side chic. One of the first models to challenge the unspoken rule that runway and photographic models were two different species, Bjornson became one of the most sought-after models in New York.

ABOVE:
BLONDE BEAUTY
A PRELIMINARY STUDY
OF KAREN BJORNSON.
NEW YORK, 1982

OPPOSITE:
CLASSIC LINES
VIRAMONTES DESCRIBED
KAREN BJORNSON AS A
'TIMELESS BEAUTY' AFTER
COMPLETING THIS PORTRAIT
OF HER FOR A *HAMPTONS*
MAGAZINE COVER IN 1980.
NEW YORK, 1980

PRINCESS GLORIA VON THURN UND TAXIS

Never one to take herself too seriously, Gloria von Thurn und Taxis stood out for both her unconventional style and devil-may-care attitude. A countess by birth and a princess by marriage, von Thurn und Taxis spent much of the 1980s swathed in a cloud of fashionable excess. It was during this time the eccentrically chic Princess earned the nickname TNT, following a *Vanity Fair* feature that labelled her 'the dynamite socialite'. With her alarmingly high coiffures and ancestral jewels she dazzled Paris, where she travelled annually to view the haute couture collections.

'I think of Tony often. He was very creative and I believe one day his work will be iconic. He was such a joy to work with. I miss him.'
JANET JACKSON

JANET JACKSON

'My first name ain't baby, it's Janet — Miss Jackson if you're nasty,' she proclaimed on the opening track of her groundbreaking album 'Control'. Until this point Jackson had been more a reflection than a pioneer, more interpreter than inventor. This album was all about Janet and establishing who she wanted to be. It was a lot sexier than any of her past albums. Tony shot the 19-year-old Jackson at Smashbox Studios in Los Angeles. He had one day to transform the former child star into an assured, fashion-forward figure with her trendsetting big hair and severe all-black ensemble.

ABOVE: POLAROIDS
BY VIRAMONTES.
LOS ANGELES, c. 1985

OPPOSITE: **REBEL REBOOT**
VIRAMONTES PROVED
HE WAS AS ADEPT AN ARTIST
WITH A CAMERA AS HE WAS
WITH A PAINTBRUSH IN THE
COVER ARTWORK FOR JANET
JACKSON'S GROUND-
BREAKING ALBUM 'CONTROL'.
LOS ANGELES, 1985.
COURTESY OF UNIVERSAL
MUSIC ENTERPRISES, A
DIVISION OF UMG
RECORDINGS, INC.

VIOLETA SANCHEZ

*'I was one of his sources of inspiration.
He loved to work with me as a base and
would then elaborate and change things.
Some of his drawings were actually
a conglomerate of all of us: my nose,
Lisa's mouth and perhaps Teri's eyes.'*

VIOLETA SANCHEZ

Before there were supermodels there was Violeta
Sanchez, a willowy stunner with a svelte figure and
runway swagger. Sanchez was born and raised in Spain,
but began her career as a model in Paris, where she
quickly caught the attention of couturiers Yves Saint
Laurent and Thierry Mugler. The latter would often
send her out first in a show just to stand at the end of
the runway and strike a pose. A study in elongated
elegance, Sanchez was glamorous in a way that we
cannot quite understand today. With her classically
elegant physique, long, fine nose and wasp-waisted
silhouette she enraptured Viramontes. Quickly
becoming his go-to face, her profile became a template,
a short-cut for summing up the strong, powerful women
that were to become his artistic stock-in-trade.

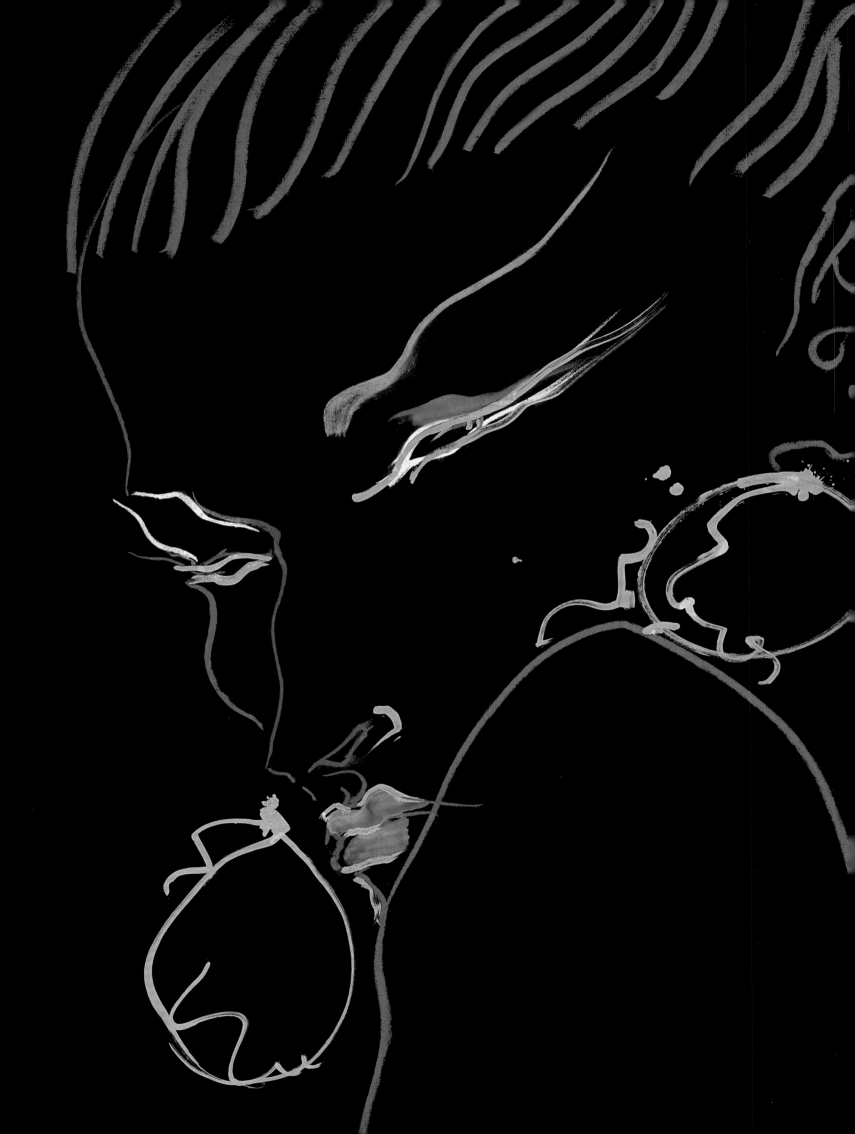

'Tony could not only talk about style, hair, make-up and art direction, he could do it all himself.'
BOB RECINE

ON MEN

'Stop wondering what others need to see. Don't be afraid to put it down on paper.'

VIRAMONTES

At a time when Ralph Lauren and Calvin Klein were peddling an image of Ivy League sobriety, Viramontes was stretching the bounds of masculine identity. Although renowned as an illustrator of women's fashion, Tony was equally at home with the male face and he produced as large a body of work celebrating the male form as the female. Ranging from portraits of friends and lovers to more provocative studies, Tony was keen to make boys look just as arresting as girls and made glossy paper stars out of a host of gorgeous young muscle boys in make-up and turbans.

Cyril Brulé, an important figure in Tony's Paris life, provided him with an endless stream of beautiful young boys to draw. Himself a former model, Brulé ran the men's division at Paris Planning and also featured in many of Tony's earliest drawings made in the French capital. 'There were a lot of similarities in the faces of the men Tony drew,' recalls Brulé. 'They were all very structured: Paul Hendrix, Brad Harryman, Jesse Harris and Mike Hill. The mouth was very important; he liked to recreate typically macho men into softer, more feminine images. Tony could take a truck driver and transform him into a drag queen. He did this very gently, he would go very slowly, it wasn't a case of "let me put some lipstick on you", he knew that would not work, but he was pushing and pushing a little further just to see how far he could go.'

Tony's relationships with his male models were far more complex and nuanced than those he maintained with his female models: Viramontes was frequently attracted to the men he drew, photographed and painted, and would often develop sexual relationships with them. However, these were characterized by heartache and frustration. Bob Recine remembers sitting up many nights listening to Tony's sorrowful tales of attraction to some boy. For, while Tony had lovers over the years, he never met his romantic soulmate. 'Tony wore his heart on his sleeve,' says Recine. 'Perhaps, in some way, he didn't feel he was worthy of a relationship. That was all part of the contradiction. He was striving for the perfect love, but I think the real love of his life was his work. Where he constantly sought to challenge the norm.'

A Pygmalion figure, Viramontes brilliantly transformed the men in his life both on paper and in person. Indeed, while women took the reins in his drawings – the so-called weaker sex becoming the stronger one – the image of the masculine role was also reversed. Tony's sensuously feline men frequently cast off their traditional, functional uniforms and become props or accessories in his drawings. Shining with grace and charm, they assume seductive poses, leaning coquett-ishly, a lewd expression in place as they gaze saucily in the viewer's direction.

After a brief casting, model Ron Grace found himself standing in Tony's Paris studio stripped to the waist and dressed in a corset and headscarf as Tony drew him. 'It was actually pretty fun,' remembers Grace, 'being from California I wasn't really used to that kinda stuff. He was definitely out there, coming at things from a different perspective. I just took it all in my stride and enjoyed my time with him.' Similarly, while working with singer Nina Hagen on a cover for German *Vogue* Viramontes brought along his sometime lover, model Mike Hill. Hagen remembers that Tony stripped Mike naked, painted his body and told her to use him as a sofa. 'The guy was very strong, so he didn't mind,' she laughs. A naked Hill made his way into many of the drawings Viramontes created for the fashion house Valentino. 'Tony was crazy about Mike Hill,' remembers Cyril Brulé, and in his work with the strapping, blonde beefcake his style reached its fullest expression.

Everyone wanted to be a Viramontes boy, remembers Bob Recine, 'it was a very distinct look that was of the moment' and one that could launch a career overnight. Tanel Bedrossiantz, muse to Jean Paul Gaultier, recalls that he was anything but the conventional male model when Tony plucked him from obscurity. 'At that time male models were Malboro Cowboys, beautiful, muscular guys with bright white teeth. I was different. I had just turned 18, I had a big mouth, big ears, the silhouette of a disjointed puppet … Tony would let me express myself in my own way, do my own thing.'

John Pearson remembers that his agent Cyril Brulé called him late one night with the news that Tony Viramontes wanted to draw him immediately for a Claude Montana campaign. Pearson, fresh from Yorkshire and with 'no understanding or sophistication of any form', confessed to Brulé that he had no idea who Claude Montana was nor did he have any idea who Tony Viramontes was. But he remembers that 'there was a buzz and energy in Cyril's voice, which convinced me it was worth doing', so he made his way across Paris to Tony's studio.

Tony's way with male models left a lasting impression, and not just on the printed page.

PAUL HENDRIX

An aspiring actor, Paul Hendrix grew up surfing on the beaches of Santa Monica, California, with ambitions to work with Franco Zeffirelli and Federico Fellini. Having made his way to Paris on the back of his matinée idol good looks, Hendrix found the fashion world there to be 'pretty wild' and felt that on occasion his eyes had been opened too much. But he concluded that it was 'much more fun than I could have found at the beach'.

PREVIOUS PAGE:
BEAUTIFUL BUTCH
THERE WERE A LOT OF
SIMILARITIES BETWEEN
THE FACES OF THE MEN
THAT VIRAMONTES DREW.
THE MOUTH WAS VERY
IMPORTANT. HERE TONY
DRAWS OUR ATTENTION TO
HENDRIX'S FULL AND
AGGRESSIVELY CURLED LIPS.
PARIS, 1984

ABOVE: POLAROIDS BY
VIRAMONTES. PARIS, c. 1984

OPPOSITE: **PAUL HENDRIX**
MEN FOUND A PLACE IN
THE FRONT AND CENTRE
OF TONY'S DRAWINGS
AND WERE AS IMPORTANT
AS WOMEN IN HIS VISUAL
VOCABULARY. PAUL
HENDRIX, DRAWN HERE
WITH A SWIFT INCISIVE
LINE, WAS A FREQUENT
SUBJECT UNTIL A BITTER
FALLING-OUT. PARIS, 1983

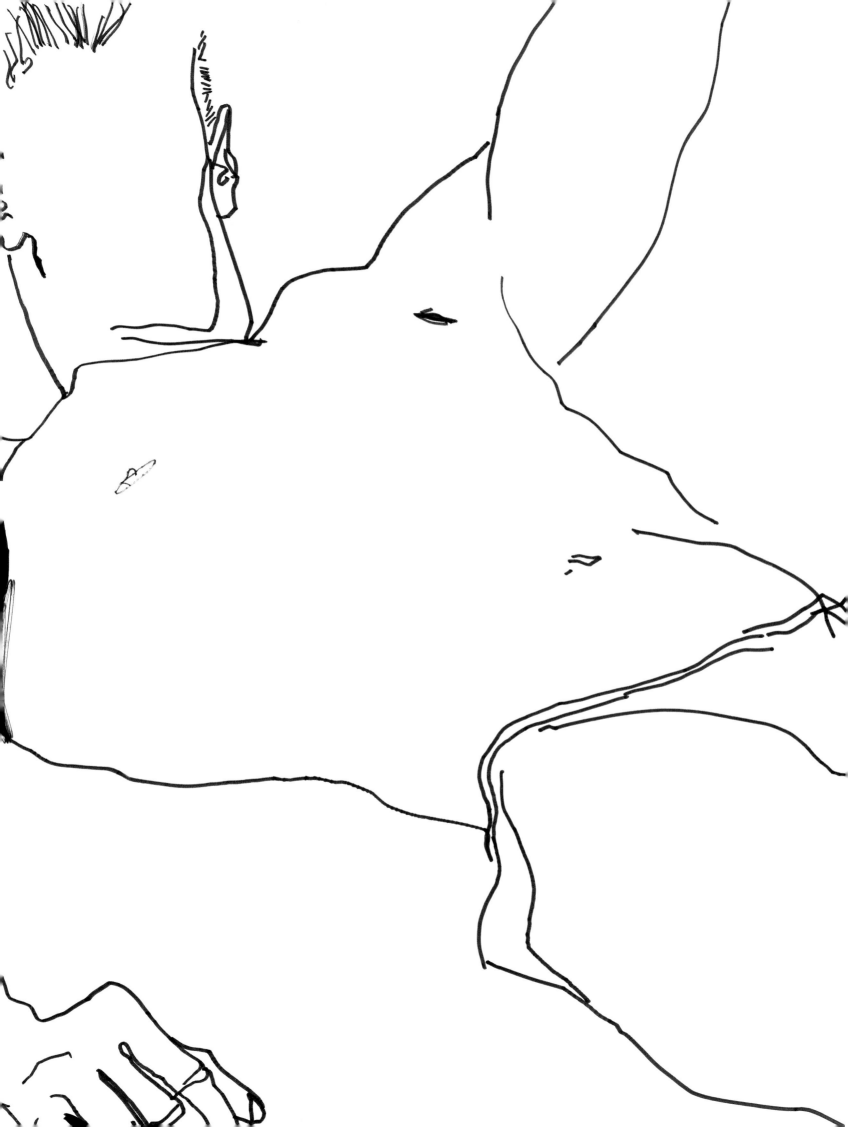

*'Before we met I had no idea how to move or create. ....
Tony opened my eyes to style and creativity, he was my education.'*
MIKE HILL

MIKE HILL

Mike Hill was a beautiful, blonde boy from Los Angeles.
Barry Kamen remembers him as 'a sweet guy, not that
bright but very sincere'. Tony met the former catalogue
model in Paris shortly after he arrived and they quickly
became lovers. It was perhaps inevitable that Hill, an
exhibitionist of the first order, would find common
cause with Viramontes, who loved to gild the lily, and
Mike swiftly became his house model. Mike was a very
commercial-looking boy, remembers Bob Recine, but
Tony fell in love with him, remade him and helped him
find his dark side. Theirs was an often volatile relationship and from that tension the work flowed, as Tony
began to articulate the tug and pull of their romance in
his drawings. Initially there was an almost savage
sensuality to the work. But gradually as their relationship ran aground, a thin line of anguish crept in, a kind
of melancholy. Hill had difficulty accepting his own
homosexuality and slowly began to pull away from Tony.
'It's not love,' Viramontes said of the relationship, 'it's an
addiction. I've become spoiled by someone who I have
gotten attached to.' As things began to deteriorate
further, Tony's lean, mean line began to glisten with a
blithe malignance.

ABOVE: POLAROID BY
VIRAMONTES. FLORIDA,
c. 1985

OPPOSITE:
COLOUR INTENSITY
TONY'S WORK REACHED
ITS FULLEST EXPRESSION
IN HIS DRAWINGS AND
PHOTOGRAPHS OF MIKE
HILL. HERE, HE EXPLORES
THE CONTOURS OF HIS FACE
IN PASTEL AND CONTÉ
CRAYON. PARIS, 1982

BUFFALO STYLE
MIKE HILL PHOTOGRAPHED
FOR *THE FACE* MAGAZINE
WITH STYLING BY RAY PETRI.
LONDON, 1985. COLLECTION
OF MITZI LORENZ

OPPOSITE:
ROMANTIC HEIGHTS
MIKE HILL IS DRESSED
TO EXCESS FOR THIS PAUL
GOBAL MAKE-UP STUDY.
PARIS, 1986

TORSO TENSION
CASUAL AND SPONTANEOUS,
VIRAMONTES RECORDS
A STATUESQUE MIKE HILL
IN COLOURED CHALKS.
PARIS, 1984

OPPOSITE: IN HIS WORK
WITH MIKE HILL,
VIRAMONTES EVOKED
A POWERFUL, SENSUOUS
AND EROTIC ATMOSPHERE.
PARIS, 1985

155

CYRIL BRULÉ

Model-turned-agent Cyril Brulé featured regularly in Tony's earliest Paris drawings. An important figure in Viramontes's life in the city, he introduced Tony to several of the men who became favourites for sketches and portraits. Brulé, who began modelling in 1981, quickly abandoned the catwalk for a desk job at Paris Planning, where he established the men's division of the agency. Instrumental in the success of many of the industry's top models, he currently helms the Paris branch of Viva Model Management, having founded the company in 1988.

MODEL MAKER
TWO FLUENT AND
EXPRESSIVE PORTRAIT
STUDIES OF MODEL
CYRIL BRULÉ REVEAL
VIRAMONTES AT HIS
MOST SIMPLE, DIRECT
AND OBSERVANT.
PARIS, 1984

FASHION EXECUTIVE
VERSACE MENSWEAR
MODELLED BY CYRIL BRULÉ.
PARIS, 1984

RIFAT OZBEK

Always darkly handsome, Rifat Ozbek arrived in London in the 1970s to study first architecture and then fashion at Saint Martin's School of Art. He had been shipped off to Liverpool University by his parents to study architecture. 'In Turkey,' he told *People* magazine, 'a man has to be either a doctor or an architect.' He made a quick change and set up his own label in 1984. Ozbek's take on his Turkish heritage brought contemporary desirability to simple, witty clothes in a *Thousand and One Nights* theme.

ABOVE: POLAROIDS BY VIRAMONTES. LONDON, 1984

OPPOSITE:
EASTERN VISION
VIRAMONTES CAPTURES A LOOK AND AN ATTITUDE WITH THIS PORTRAIT OF THE DESIGNER. LONDON, 1984

RON GRACE

A California native, Ron Grace entered the fashion world rather nonchalantly after being spotted at a friend's wedding. He soon found himself with an agent and began working regularly with photographer Bruce Weber on a series of Calvin Klein campaigns.

CALIFORNIA DREAMER
DELINEATED IN BROAD
BLACK BRUSHSTROKES,
TWO STUDIES OF MODEL
RON GRACE. PARIS, 1986

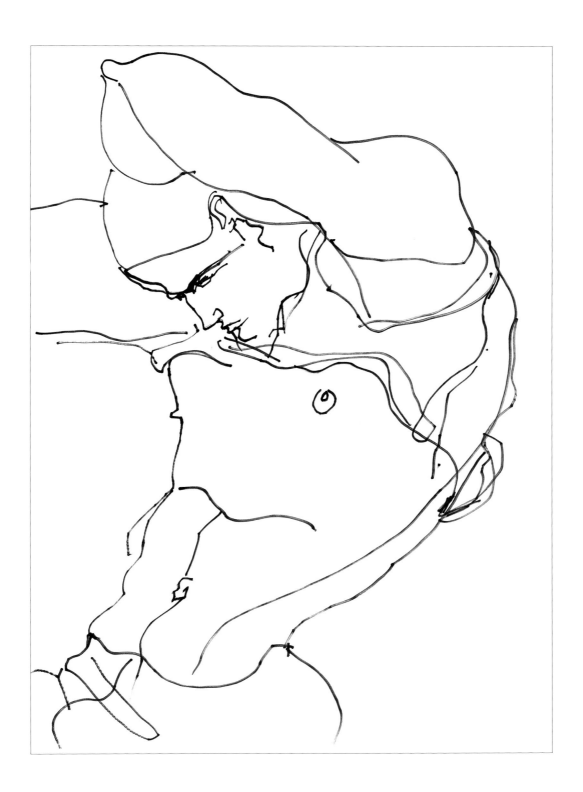

JESSE HARRIS

Anyone who passed Tony's door might find themselves drawn into his work and Jesse Harris, the face of countless Versace campaigns, proved himself to be flavour of the moment. Always keen to keep his regular boys – Mike Hill, Brad Harryman and Paul Hendrix – on their toes, Viramontes turned to Harris for a time in 1984 and produced a series of beautifully realised portrait sketches of this American in Paris.

ANATOMICALLY CORRECT FASCINATED WITH ANATOMY, TONY DREW IT OBSESSIVELY. HERE HE OBSERVES JESSE HARRIS WITH TYPICAL ECONOMY OF LINE. PARIS, 1984

OPPOSITE AND OVERLEAF: VIRAMONTES'S VITAL BRUSHWORK ENLIVENS PORTRAITS OF HARRIS IN THIS COMMISSION FOR ITALIAN TEXTILE GIANT GOMATEX. PARIS, 1984

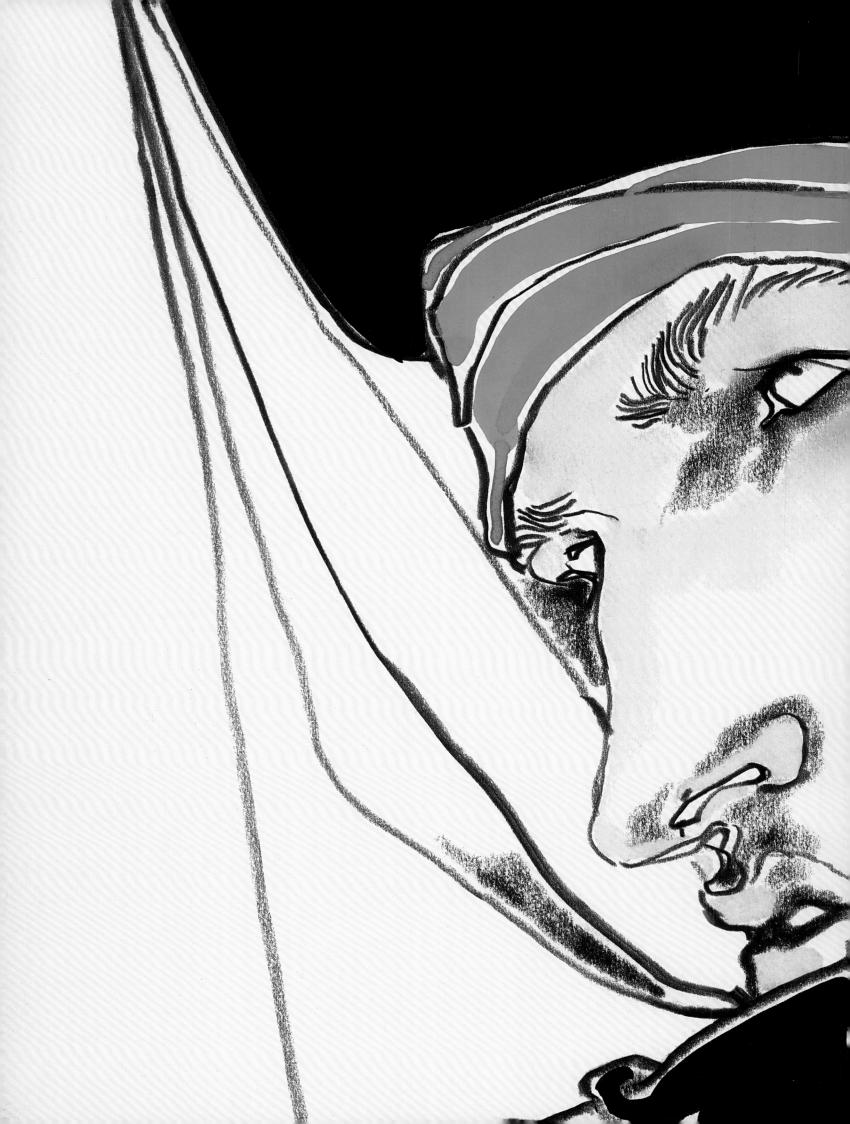

IDEAL MEN

Always on the lookout for the perfect face,
Viramontes had a particularly high strike rate.
His sketchbooks are populated with dozens of simple
yet spirited drawings of anonymous faces
and models who have since fallen into obscurity.

NICK ALEXANDER
PARIS, 1983

OPPOSITE: **DAVID HORI**
NEW YORK, 1986

HOUSE MODEL
RAY PETRI SERVED AS
THE MODEL FOR THIS
STYLIZED SLEEVE ART
FOR PHIL PICKETT'S 1984
OLYMPIC THEME, 'DESTINY'.
LONDON, 1984. COLLECTION
OF MITZI LORENZ

OPPOSITE:
THE SARTORIALIST
A POWERFUL PORTRAIT
OF RAY PETRI IN HIS
SIGNATURE PORK PIE HAT.
LONDON, 1984

RAY PETRI

Leading stylist Ray Petri set the alternative agenda in the 1980s with his Buffalo label, a mix of high street and high fashion looks that appeared in *i-D*, *The Face* and *Arena*. Combining influences from boxing culture, Jamaican Raggamuffins and rude boys to punks to create a tough androgynous look, he was perhaps the first person to turn the selection and editing of clothes into a profession. He was also one of the first to champion mixed-race models, including Nick Kamen. Born in Scotland but raised in Brisbane, Australia, Petri arrived in London in 1969 and was soon working with fashion photographers Marc Lebon and Jamie Morgan. Petri pioneered putting men in skirts and women in baggy suits; his personal uniform was black jeans, bomber jacket and pork pie hat.

'For me fashion was like art, a way to express myself.
Tony made me. I learned how to use myself to control my image,
to give the best I can give.'
TANEL BEDROSSIANTZ

TANEL BEDROSSIANTZ

Viramontes ignited the career of Tanel Bedrossiantz
effortlessly, after discovering him in the wardrobe
department of a studio in which he was shooting.
Realizing he had more in common with the female
models of the moment, Bedrossiantz began to study
and recreate their poses, to the delight of Viramontes.
'I knew that I had to do something different for people
to see me,' he says. Tanel's first shoot with Viramontes
was to have a dramatic impact, changing his life
completely as Jean Paul Gaultier chose him to front
a campaign, and a host of international designers
requested he walk in their shows.

ABOVE: POLAROID BY
VIRAMONTES. PARIS, c. 1985

OPPOSITE:
MODEL BEHAVIOUR
TANEL BEDROSSIANTZ SHOT
BY VIRAMONTES FOR PER
LUI. PARIS, 1985

GREG
THOMPSON

Viramontes began drawing Greg Thompson at Steven Meisel's illustration classes in the late 1970s and continued to do so throughout his life. Not a professional model, and with no interest in becoming one, Thompson worked as a graphic designer and was known primarily for his physique. 'Greg had an amazing body,' remembers Bob Recine. 'I think that was Tony's initial interest and inspiration in drawing him, but Greg was also a beautiful human being, a bit on the quiet side, but very calm and friendly.' Thompson was a regular visitor to Viramontes's Paris apartment and the two enjoyed a long-standing on-again off-again romantic relationship.

ABOVE: POLAROIDS BY VIRAMONTES. NEW YORK, c. 1980

OPPOSITE:
COMPLEMENTARY COLOURS
A MASTER OF DIVERSE DRAWING TECHNIQUES, VIRAMONTES CONTRASTS BRIGHTS WITH REALISTIC SKIN TONE IN THIS PORTRAIT. NEW YORK, 1982

SUITED AND BOOTED
GREG THOMPSON MODELS
VERSACE MENSWEAR.
NEW YORK, 1984

BRAD HARRYMAN

As American as apple pie, Brad Harryman was perhaps the most commercially successful of all Tony's boys. Standing at 6' 1" the blonde-haired, blue-eyed hunk was a natural choice to front campaigns for labels such as Mugler and Valentino. Harryman was one of the most familiar faces in fashion editorials across the world in the 1980s before his premature death in 2000.

PHOTO-COLLAGE OF BRAD HARRYMAN. PARIS, 1985

OPPOSITE:

HUNK HARRYMAN
THE MAGIC OF VIRAMONTES'S BRUSH BRINGS ALIVE THE TENSION IN HARRYMAN'S NECK IN THIS SKETCHBOOK STUDY. PARIS, 1986

WAY BANDY

Bandy began life in Birmingham, Alabama, as plain old Ronald Wright, a married high school English teacher. He arrived in New York in the summer of 1965 and chose to stay, reinventing himself with a new name, a new career and a new nose. 'The minute I arrived I knew I would never go back to my former life,' he told a reporter in 1978. 'This was a new beginning, I felt compelled to become Way Bandy, the name just came into my consciousness.' While his wife returned to Alabama, Bandy the 'freelance face designer' went on to perform his magic on some of the world's most celebrated women. He accented what he called Catherine Deneuve's 'extraordinary face' and changed Elizabeth Taylor's eye shadow from blue to brown. 'If it launched a thousand ships, the face was probably done up by make-up genius Way Bandy,' declared *People* magazine. His idealized cover girls with their dewy translucent skin and glossy red lips defined notions of glamour for close to two decades. Bandy died in 1988 and was one of the first high-profile victims of the disease to ask that his death be announced as AIDS-related.

ABOVE: POLAROIDS BY VIRAMONTES. FLORIDA, c. 1981

OPPOSITE:
MAKE-UP BELIEVE
IN THIS COLOUR-WASH SKETCH, BANDY LOOKS AS GLAMOROUS AS THE WOMEN HE MADE UP. FLORIDA, 1985

SHARP LOOKS
NICK KAMEN PHOTO-
GRAPHED FOR *PER LUI*.
TONY'S PHOTOGRAPHIC
WORK SHARED MANY
CHARACTERISTICS OF HIS
DRAWINGS, AND WAS
ALWAYS RECONGIZABLY
VIRAMONTES. PARIS, 1984

NICK KAMEN

One of the few mixed-race models working in London
during the early 1980s, Nick Kamen had gone into
modelling with little conviction and even less success
until stylist Ray Petri featured him on the front cover
of *The Face*. With his jet-black hair, pale brown skin
and soft blue-green eyes Kamen quickly became an
overnight celebrity and soon abandoned the catwalk
for pop superstardom.

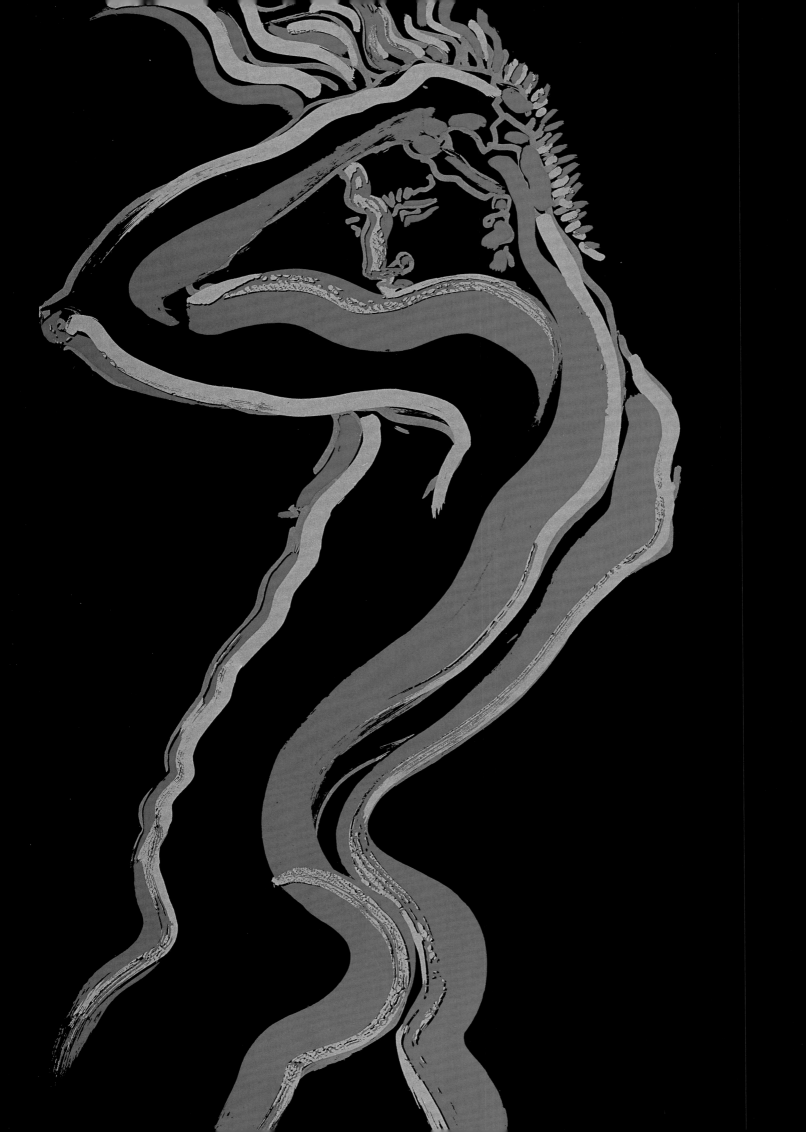

'It was just like you imagine Jackson Pollock did with painting. I was there for about 20 minutes and I heard paper ripping constantly and afterwards he said, "That's great. We're finished".'

JOHN PEARSON

JOHN PEARSON

John Pearson was just beginning his career when he posed for Viramontes in 1984. 'I had no idea where the hell I was going, I think it was about midnight when I got there. I was quite tentative about what to expect but I found his studio, it was very dark and a little scary. I was just this Yorkshire boy venturing into a cave of Sodom and Gomorrah, this Mecca of creative, frenzied homosexual energy. I saw Tony, whom I towered over, and he looked me up and down before handing me a gold lamé G-string. My immediate, over-masculine reaction was to say "it's not big enough" – it was the first thing that came out of my mouth, so another was quickly produced. I then had to stand on a podium in a G-string and start posing. It was the first time I had ever been drawn. There was no conversation apart from the little direction Tony gave me: arch your back more, stretch out your body. … It was the first time I saw myself on posters and when I got to New York I was able to say I did the Claude Montana campaign.'

ABOVE: POLAROID BY VIRAMONTES. PARIS, 1986

OPPOSITE: **BLUE NUDE** SENSUOUSLY FELINE, JOHN PEARSON SHINES WITH GRACE AND CHARM IN THE BROAD BRUSHSTROKES OF THIS PAINTING FOR MONTANA MENSWEAR. PARIS, 1986. COURTESY OF CLAUDE MONTANA

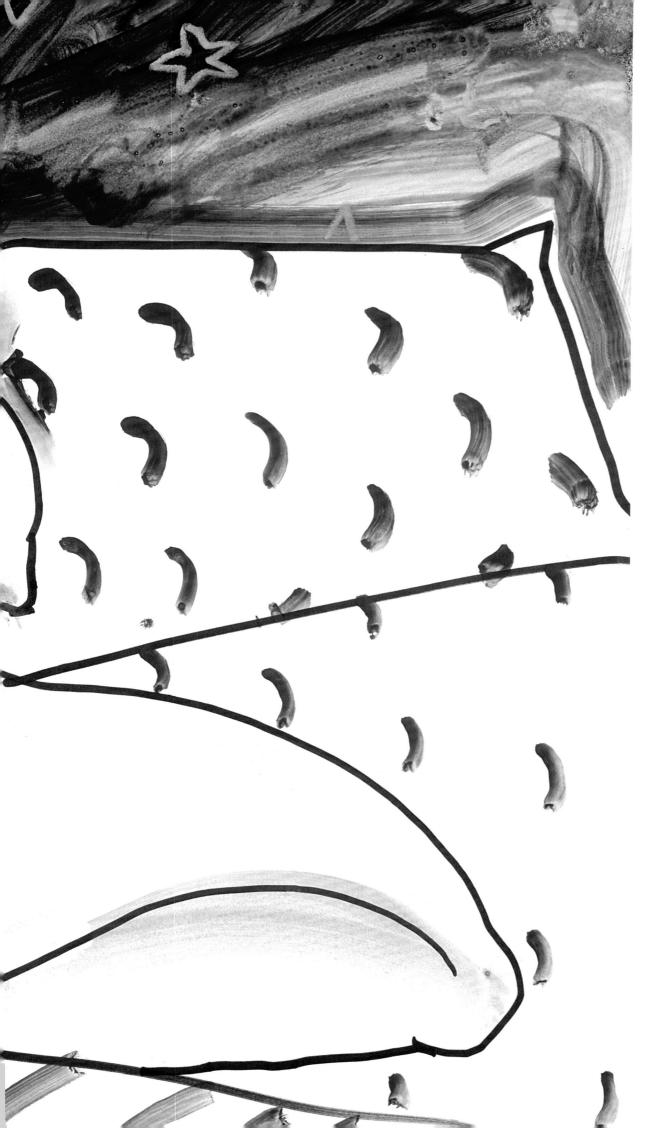

LARS SLEEPING
A NATURAL OBSERVER,
VIRAMONTES RECORDED
HIS LOVER SLEEPING
IN THIS TEASING, EROTIC
AND PAINTERLY STUDY.
PARIS, 1984

189

AFTERWORD BY
AMY FINE
COLLINS

As digital technology has transformed the photograph into raw material for manipulation, and nearly everyone into a photographer, the taste for hand-drawn fashion illustration has finally returned. In *Vanity Fair* we now regularly see the exquisite, dreamy renderings of David Downton. Christian Dior Beauty has its own artist in residence, Bil Donovan. And an iPad app sometimes used for on-the-spot runway sketching, 'Paper by 53', has won an Apple award.

So, thankfully, we once again have a receptive audience for the oeuvre of Tony Viramontes, in my view an '80s Egon Schiele to Antonio's more suave Gustav Klimt. Ludwig Bemelmans, creator of the Madeline storybooks, observed that a good illustration should be composed with alacrity, instantaneity and facility, so that it 'sits on paper as if you smacked a spoon of whipped cream on a plate'. Viramontes's drawings instead streak like hot cinders across the page, where they continue to glow and smoulder.

Amy Fine Collins
New York, 2013

'I want to make a statement.
I want to explore myself on paper,
canvas, film. I feel so much better
when I draw – paint –
just use my artistic talent.'
VIRAMONTES, 1979

TONY VIRAMONTES
SELF PORTRAIT. PARIS, 1986

ACKNOWLEDGEMENTS

My first debt of gratitude is to David Downton, who planted the seed for this book and introduced me to Tony's older brother Ed Viramontes, godfather of the project. Ed, without your unerring assistance, advice and encouragement this book would certainly not have been started, let alone completed.

A special thank you must go to Laurence King for acknowledging the need to chronicle Tony's contribution to the world of fashion illustration, and Helen Rochester who commissioned this book. Susie May, thank you for patiently guiding me through the day-to-day production of this project and allowing me the time to shape this manuscript.

I would also like to thank Michael Setek of art4site. Michael was indispensible, masterminding the scanning, retouching and digital restoration of Tony's original artwork. I am deeply indebted to you for your continued help and support.

Many people assisted in the creation of this book by sharing memories, making introductions and reading drafts. But I could not possibly have found my way if it had not been for the amazing Susann Güenther, perhaps Tony's closest friend, confidante and keeper of the flame. Susann guided me through Tony's professional life and Parisian adventures with great aplomb and was always more encouraging than strictly necessary. I count her as an ally on this project. Similarly, Sylvana Castres, perhaps the best-connected woman in Paris, shared her invaluable contacts, making sure I met as many members of Tony's extended group of friends as possible.

For their time, knowledge and professional insight I am particularly indebted to Frédérique Lorca, Tanel Bedrossiantz and Cyril Brulé, who gave generously of their time and were nothing but supportive and encouraging. Bob Recine remembered absolutely everything and withheld nothing.

Special thanks go to photographer Armin Weisheit for being a white knight and travelling to Paris with me at the drop of a hat to shoot many of the images Tony created for Valentino. There are no words to thank Jean Paul Gaultier for his contribution in taking the time to write the foreword for this book. Amy Fine Collins's afterword beautifully encapsulates the present and timeless appeal of Tony's work. Thank you, Amy.

I am particularly grateful to all those who so graciously allowed me to strip artwork from their walls; to all the photographers and designers who rummaged through their archives to find just the right images; to those who generously provided me with these materials, often without charge. At Condé Nast I must thank Lucinda Chambers, Anna Harvey, Brett Croft, Shawn Waldron, Raineri Paola and Bonnie Robinson. At the Valentino Archives librarian Hervé Goraud-Mounier and Jasmine Habeler were both particularly proactive, going well beyond the call of duty. My sincere thanks to Nick Rhodes for giving so freely of his time and making available many previously unpublished drawings by Tony from his own private collection. Madame Yasuko Suita at The Hanae Mori Foundation turned up all manner of forgotten treasures. Sean Rose Roderik at Universal Music Ltd helped cut through a forest of red tape and allowed me to publish Tony's portraits of Janet Jackson.

The list of those to thank is long and inevitably I have left people out; my apologies to those I have overlooked. But thanks are also due to the following: **In Paris** Claude and Jaqueline Montana, Valentino Garavani, Giancarlo Giammetti, Bernard Pesce, Beatrice Paul, Leslie Winer, Sibylle de Saint Phalle, Brigitte Slama, Jean Jacques Castres, Marc Ascoli, Claudia Huidobro, Christine Bergstrom, BillyBoy* & Lala, Patrick Sarfati, Thierry Perez, Violeta Sanchez, Eugenia Melian, Ignacio Garza. **In London** Barry Kamen, Jamie Morgan, Robert Forrest, Mitzi Lorenz, Scarlett Cannon, Armin Weisheit. **In Rome** Franca Sozzani, Princess Gloria von Thurn und Taxis, Anna Piaggi, Valdettaro Violante. **In Milan** Francesca Spiller and Carla at Galleria Carla Sozzani. **In New York** Jeremiah Goodman, Betty Eng, Lisa Rosen, Lisa Rubenstein, Karen Bjornson MacDonald, Mao Padilha, James Aguiar, Mark Haldeman, Teri Toye, Michael H. Berkowitz, Nicholas Manville, Paul Caranicas, Sophie de Taillac, Ben Shaul, Doug and Gene Meyer, Polly Mellen, Freddie Leiba, James Breese, William 'Bil' Donovan, Charles 'Chuck' Nitzberg, Randal Meyers, J. Alexander, Desmond Cadogan, Carlos Taylor, Wendy Whitelaw, Giovanna Calabretta, and Bobby Butz. **In Los Angeles** Anita, Ralph, Kathy and Manuel Viramontes, Leonard Stanley, Nicky Butler, Julie Rosenbaum, Janet Jackson, René Russo and Janice Dickinson. **In Japan** Madame Hanae Mori, Mariko Kohga.

Michael H. Berkowitz, thank you for sharing your encyclopaedic knowledge of the fashion world's comings and goings so willingly and Paul Huntley, my ever gracious landlord, for providing me with a home away from home at his Manhattan castle.

And finally on a more personal note, thanks to my helpful and long-suffering friend Emma Denholm, who while bolstering me with optimism nonetheless acted as a ruthlessly tactless critic of my prose, helping me clean everything up and making sure I said exactly what I wanted to say.

BIBLIOGRAPHY

The text in *Viramontes* was composed using extracts from the diaries of Tony Viramontes and interviews with his friends and associates, along with materials from The Hanae Mori Foundation in Japan and the Valentino Garavani Archives in Paris. The following books provided additional background information.

Blackman, Cally, *100 Years of Fashion Illustration*
(London: Laurence King, 2007)

Borrelli, Laird, *Stylishly Drawn*
(New York: Abrams, 2000)

Chenoune, Farid, *Yves Saint Laurent*
(New York: Abrams, 2010)

Drake, Nicholas, *Fashion Illustration Today*
(London: Thames and Hudson, 1987)

Downton, David, *Masters of Fashion Illustration*
(London: Laurence King, 2010)

Downton, David (ed.), *Pourqoi Pas? A Journal of Fashion Illustration*, Issue Two (London, 2008)

Gross, Michael, *Model: The Ugly Business of Beautiful Women* (New York: Warner Books, 1996)

Jones, Stephen et al., *Stephen Jones & The Accent of Fashion* (Tielt, Belgium: Lannoo, 2010)

Junji, Itoh, *Viramontes* (Japan: Ryuko Tsushin, 1988)

Martin, Richard, *Fashion and Surrealism*
(London: Thames and Hudson, 1989)

McMullan, Patrick, *So 80s: A Photographic Diary of a Decade* (New York: PowerHouse Books, 2003)

Menkes, Suzy and Nathalie Bondil, *The Fashion Universe of Jean Paul Gaultier: From the Street to the Stars* (New York: Abrams, 2011)

Mori, Hanae, *Hanae Mori: Highlights from a Lifetime in Fashion* (Japan: Kodanska, 2001)

Packer, William, *Fashion Drawing in Vogue*
(London: Thames and Hudson, 1983)

Padilha, Mauricio and Robert Padhilha,
The Stephen Sprouse Book (New York: Rizzoli, 2009)

Tyrnauer, Matt, *Valentino* (Italy: Taschen, 2007)

Voss, Ursula, *Art Fashion* (Volker & Ingrid Zahm, 2003)

tony Vincin tes